S0-AFR-828

3-MINUTE
DEVOTIONS
FOR THE WORKPLACE

© 2017 by Barbour Publishing, Inc.

Edited by and prayers written by Ed Strauss.

Print ISBN 978-1-68322-237-8

All rights reserved. No part of this publication may be reproduced or transmitted for commercial purposes, except for brief quotations in printed reviews, without written permission of the publisher.

Churches and other noncommercial interests may reproduce portions of this book without the express written permission of Barbour Publishing, provided that the text does not exceed 500 words or 5 percent of the entire book, whichever is less, and that the text is not material quoted from another publisher. When reproducing text from this book, include the following credit line: "From *3-Minute Devotions for the Workplace*, published by Barbour Publishing, Inc. Used by permission."

All scripture quotations, unless otherwise noted, are taken from the King James Version of the Bible.

Scripture quotations marked NIV are taken from the HOLY BIBLE, NEW INTERNATIONAL VERSION®. NIV®. Copyright © 1973, 1978, 1984, 2011 by Biblica, Inc.™ Used by permission. All rights reserved worldwide.

Scripture quotations marked NKJV are taken from the New King James Version®. Copyright © 1982 by Thomas Nelson, Inc. Used by permission. All rights reserved.

Scripture quotations marked NLT are taken from the *Holy Bible*. New Living Translation copyright© 1996, 2004, 2015 by Tyndale House Foundation. Used by permission of Tyndale House Publishers, Inc. Carol Stream, Illinois 60188. All rights reserved.

Scripture quotations marked AMPC are taken from the Amplified® Bible, Classic Edition © 1954, 1958, 1962, 1964, 1965, 1987 by The Lockman Foundation. Used by permission.

Scripture quotations marked NASB are taken from the New American Standard Bible, © 1960, 1962, 1963, 1968, 1971, 1972, 1973, 1975, 1977, 1995 by The Lockman Foundation. Used by permission.

Published by Barbour Books, an imprint of Barbour Publishing, Inc., P.O. Box 719, Uhrichsville, Ohio 44683, www.barbourbooks.com

Our mission is to publish and distribute inspirational products offering exceptional value and biblical encouragement to the masses.

Member of the
Evangelical Christian
Publishers Association

Printed in the United States of America.

3-MINUTE DEVOTIONS

DEVOTIONS

FOR THE WORKPLACE

180 Inspiring Readings

BARBOUR BOOKS
An Imprint of Barbour Publishing, Inc.

INTRODUCTION

Most days we're seeking out a moment or two of inspiration and encouragement—a fresh breath of air for the lungs and soul.

Here is a collection of moments from the true Source of all inspiration and encouragement—God's Word. Within these pages you'll be guided through just-right-size readings that you can experience in as few as three minutes:

- Minute 1: Reflect on God's Word

- Minute 2: Read real-life application and encouragement

- Minute 3: Pray

These devotions aren't meant to be a replacement for digging deep into the scriptures or for personal, in-depth quiet time. Instead, consider them a perfect jump-start to help you form a habit of spending time with God every day. Or add them to the time you're already spending with Him. Share these moments with friends, family, coworkers, and others you come in contact with every day. They're looking for inspiration and encouragement, too.

Your word is a lamp to guide my feet and a light for my path.
PSALM 119:105 NLT

GOD'S WORK

And I have filled him with the spirit of God, in wisdom,
and in understanding, and in knowledge, and in all
manner of workmanship, To devise cunning works,
to work in gold, and in silver, and in brass.

EXODUS 31:3-4

* * *

God thinks highly of a good worker. He even gives people the ability to do their work well. This passage shows us that when it describes Bezaleel, whom God especially gifted so that he could make all the metal things the priests would put in the temple's Holy of Holies.

Have you ever treated your work as sacred to God? Imagine if every day you were crafting something for God's most holy place. Would that make you think differently about welding together that metal, serving that customer, typing up that report, or balancing those books? Would you feel as if your work was suddenly much more important?

The fact is that each of us is working for God. He has given us our abilities, put us in our workplaces, and placed His Spirit in our hearts. When we serve others for Him, no matter what our job titles or pay scales, we are doing the most important labor of all—God's work.

Lord, thank You for giving me this work.
Show me how to do Your work every moment on my job.

A DAY EACH WEEK

Six days thou shalt labour, and do all thy work:
But the seventh day is the sabbath of the
LORD thy God: in it thou shalt not do any work.

DEUTERONOMY 5:13–14

* * *

Workaholics, beware! Don't expect God to sanction your seven-day workweek.

God did not mean our jobs to be everyday things. We wear out emotionally and spiritually if we focus continuously on work. Worse than that, it quickly becomes our god. When we become too wrapped up in our careers, the place He is designed for—the center of our lives—becomes filled with thoughts of how we can cram more labor into our days, get things done, and improve our status in the company. Before long, we're empty and tired. We've been grasping at straws, and suddenly we find a hayrack in our hands, not the success we'd looked for.

Life without God is empty. So take a day of rest, worship God, and get your life in focus. Give God His proper place, and life will go more smoothly. You'll find success, even if it's not in the place you expected it.

Lord, I need to keep You in the center of my life.
Help me spend one day each week worshipping You,
not the things I "need" to accomplish.

TURN TO GOD

The righteous cry, and the LORD heareth,
and delivereth them out of all their troubles.

PSALM 34:17

* * *

Overwhelming pressure—your boss just handed you a big project and a tight deadline. *No way can I do this!* your mind immediately cries.

Don't give up yet. You haven't even begun to tap into the power that can make it happen: you haven't turned to God. Coworkers may not be able to solve your problem, but God still has it all in control. The One who created this world and knows just how it is designed bends a listening ear to your troubles when you open your heart to Him. With His help, you may find solutions to your problems that amaze you. What once seemed so hard can flow easily when blessed by His hand.

But whether the job goes smoothly or stumbles to a halt, with God it will all work out. So place your trust in Him. He hasn't forgotten this Bible verse. He promised to get you out of all your troubles, and He'll deliver you from this one, too.

Lord, though I know You want to help when I'm in trouble, I often look to myself for answers. Instead, help me turn quickly to You. Thank You for caring about every little piece of my life.

EMPTY SUCCESS

Fret not thyself because of evildoers, neither be
thou envious against the workers of iniquity.

PSALM 37:1

* * *

Your dishonest coworker seems to move quickly up the ladder, while your pace is slowed. Yet no one seems to notice his lack of ethics—or care about it.

Don't give in and wander down his quick-success path, because success that comes quickly can also disappear in a moment. That fast-track coworker may achieve all his goals, only to find that his hands are empty. All he worked for really meant nothing in the end.

Sometimes God lets evil people be successful because they will never achieve anything but worldly success. Either He can use that empty success to lead them to Himself or use it to close their mouths on complaints against Him when they come to their barren end. Either way, the things God allows the wicked to do will be used to His purposes.

Whatever happens, evil's not the path God has for you. Don't make yourself spiritually empty because you looked only for success. Instead of following evildoers, follow God.

Lord, it's so hard to see wicked people grab so much of the
good things in this world. Remind me that I can expect
more than everything this world has to offer.
Keep my eyes on Your eternal reward.

BLESSING WITH BLESSINGS

And I have given you a land for which ye did not labour,
and cities which ye built not, and ye dwell in them; of the
vineyards and oliveyards which ye planted not do ye eat.

JOSHUA 24:13

❀ ❀ ❀

Sometimes things come easily to us. The work seems to go smoothly, and the rewards seem even larger than we expected. *What, am I on a roll?* we may want to ask ourselves.

No, it's not a roll; it's a time of blessing. Sometimes God just seems to let us have so much, we wonder why He's doing it. Life seems wonderful, and we can enjoy it. But we can't forget that all this blessing has a purpose. God doesn't give a promotion without expecting we'll use our new position wisely. He doesn't give raises that He expects us to spend only on ourselves; we need to remember the work of His church and give accordingly.

Feeling blessed? Have you asked God what you can do to share that blessing? Then, have you done what He commanded?

Thank You, Lord, for the many blessings You've given me.
Today show me how to use the ones in my hand now.

HUMBLE AGENTS

*Because thine heart was tender, and thou didst
humble thyself before God. . .and weep before me;
I have even heard thee also, saith the Lord.*

2 CHRONICLES 34:27

* * *

God loves to listen to humble people—whether they're CEOs or on the cleanup staff.

Josiah was at the top of his organization; he was king of Judah. But when the high priest found the scriptures Judah had ignored and forgotten, the humble king realized how far his country was from God's Word and the Father's will. Josiah didn't make excuses or avoid the truth. While grieving over that sin, Josiah recognized God's right to judge all Judah. He confessed his country's sin to God, and God heard. God didn't save the country, but He saved the king by bringing him home to Himself before the judgment fell.

Just as God listened to a humble king's prayer, He listens to humble workers today. When your company seems to be going in the wrong direction, maybe He has put you there to be the unobtrusive prayer. He may use you as an agent for change, or He may move you out of that bad spot, as He did Josiah. But He will hear your prayer.

*Lord, make me Your agent in my workplace.
I want to serve You every day.*

STAND UP!

"But my righteous one will live by faith.
And I take no pleasure in the one who shrinks back."
HEBREWS 10:38 NIV

* * *

Stacy knew Ken hadn't been responsible for the incorrect information that had cost her company an important contract. She wasn't sure who had made the mistake, but because she and Ken had worked so closely on the project, she knew he had done everything thoroughly and was being unfairly blamed. Why, she'd been there when their boss had gone over the work and commended him for a fine job. But Rob had retired last month and could not speak up for Ken.

What should I do? Stacy asked herself. There was a real flap on about this. Her new boss might not like her interfering in it. But the more Stacy prayed, the more certain she was that she had to defend her coworker. It was the right thing to do. A little timidly, she confronted her boss with the information and asked him to pass it on.

When Ken was cleared of all wrongdoing, Stacy was glad she had not held her tongue. If she hadn't stepped forward in faith, what would have happened to her coworker?

Lord, when I need to stand up for You
and the truth, give me the courage I need.

DRUDGERY DAYS

And let us not be weary in well doing:
for in due season we shall reap, if we faint not.

GALATIANS 6:9

✳ ✳ ✳

We all have those days when work seems so dull, we wonder if we really like our jobs anymore and why we got into them. Is it all a big mistake? Has God changed His mind about where we're headed?

When life has lost its zip, it's time to take a look at where you are. Is it the dull winter weather that's making you feel bored? Is it a lack of challenge in your job? Do you need to take some time away from work, perhaps a vacation or just a day off? Lots of things contribute to our drudgery days.

But one thing we cannot stop doing—we cannot stop doing good in Jesus' name, on the job and off. No matter what the cause of our drudgery, if we reconnect to God and follow His commands about our situation, He will help us find a way out—one that will not leave us feeling bored and useless.

When we stick with it, we will reap an unexpected harvest. God has promised it.

Lord, when I start to feel tired of work and the world,
fill me with Your Spirit and help me move on in You.

LONG-TERM SECURITY

Those who trust in the LORD are like Mount Zion,
which cannot be shaken but endures forever.

PSALM 125:1 NIV

* * *

Are things looking up for your company, or are they looking mighty grim?

Most of us expect our companies to provide security. We all want good, secure jobs. But when a company starts looking precarious, we worry about the future and may even start looking for another "good, secure job."

Our incomes keep us alive, so of course job security concerns us. We want to pay the rent and grocery bills and can't do it if we don't work. But when we place all our trust in companies, we'll experience disappointment. CEOs can't predict the financial future, hard as they try. Managers can't be certain our positions won't be axed in a corporate downsize.

But when we look to God for security, we will never be shaken. He knows the future. He foresees what jobs we need, long before we find them. Even if we lose our jobs unexpectedly, He helps us pay the rent and put food on the table.

Today, are you trusting in a short-term business or an eternal Father?

Thank You, Lord, that I can trust in Your eternal care.
I place my future in Your hands.

TOUGH LOVE

If it be possible, as much as lieth in you,
live peaceably with all men.

ROMANS 12:18

❋ ❋ ❋

"I hate to say it, but I can't stand Vera! She's awful at her job, but none of the bosses know it. We have to pick up her slack, and she isn't even nice about it! To top it off, now she's getting a promotion," Liz fumed to her husband. "How can they promote such a mean, incompetent person?"

There's frequently one person who's impossible to get along with in your work environment. You try and try, but somehow you can't create a relationship that truly works. Whether that person is nasty or conniving, you'd just rather not share your space with her.

God tells you to make every effort. Be nice when she's nasty. Show His love over and over. Don't get involved in the work "gossip pool." But ultimately, if everything you do doesn't work, don't take responsibility for all her issues. If she insists on being nasty, you can't change her attitude. Don't stop loving her as much as you can, but don't let her take complete advantage of you, either. Be a testimony, but not a pushover.

Lord, help me deal lovingly with that tough person in my job,
but also guard me from the hurt that she can cause.

GOD KNOWS

So then, each of us will give an account of ourselves to God.

ROMANS 14:12 NIV

* * *

Ever felt like playing hooky from work? The weather is beautiful. Who would know if you called in sick and spent the day having some fun?

Your boss might never figure it out. It might not matter to your work, if you weren't too busy. It might not even cost you a raise or promotion. But God would know. In lying about your situation, you would be letting Him down.

So what will it matter to God? you might ask.

If you called in and asked for a last-minute vacation day, assuming your company's policy allowed that, it wouldn't be a problem. God isn't a spoilsport. But remember, you are working for Him, too. If you call in sick and no one catches on that it was really a *slick* day, at the end of time you'll still have to give an account to God for your lack of truthfulness. Then it won't seem so slick anymore. Instead it will seem like an unnecessary lie. Why face God with any more of them than you have to?

Even when the weather calls me, Lord, help me to be responsible. I don't want to hurt You by being less than honest.

RELATIONSHIP BUSTERS

A gossip separates close friends.

PROVERBS 16:28 NIV

• • •

If you've ever had someone gossip about you, you know why this verse is in the Bible. Put a bunch of people together in the same office or on the same job site, and sooner or later the whispering starts. "Did you hear about . . .?" "I heard that Mary . . ." People just can't seem to resist talking about one another.

What may start out as "innocent information" can quickly damage reputations and cause hurt among friends. It can destroy even a close friendship. God warns against gossip because it breaks relationships. He doesn't care if it's "true gossip" or a pack of lies—spreading news about other people is not part of the biblical code.

So when you hear something that you "just have to tell" someone, put one hand over your mouth, bite your tongue, or do whatever you must to keep your mouth shut. Ask God to give you self-control, because you don't want to break up a relationship—especially your relationship with Him.

Lord, place Your hand over my mouth when
I hear that juicy bit of gossip, and help me
turn away from the one who's telling that tale.

POWERFUL FOOLISHNESS

For the message of the cross is foolishness to those who are
perishing, but to us who are being saved it is the power of God.
1 CORINTHIANS 1:18 NIV

* * *

You may work in a rough environment, where people continually
take the Lord's name in vain, or your more sophisticated coworkers
may act as if believing in Jesus is the ultimate act of foolishness.
However they show it, people who don't believe in Jesus live out
the first part of this verse. No matter what they *say* about their
own religious observances, somehow their actions show where
their hearts really are.

Every person's heart shows what's inside by words, actions,
and reactions to uncontrollable situations. Often, you don't have to
start up a conversation about faith to learn that. How often have you
recognized another believer on the job just because of his attitude
or her quiet spirit? God's power simply shines through that person.

When people think the cross is foolish, foolishness shows up
in their lives, one way or another. When they trust in God's power
for salvation, it works within them day by day, working a powerful
change in their lives.

Today, is your life foolish or powerful?

Lord, help me understand why people think
You are foolishness, but help me reach out, too.

HONEST WORK

Slaves, obey your earthly masters in everything; and do it,
not only when their eye is on you and to curry their favor,
but with sincerity of heart and reverence for the Lord.

COLOSSIANS 3:22 NIV

* * *

Harry really hustled when the boss was standing over him but eased off as soon as he passed by. That act might have fooled his boss, but Harry's coworkers quickly caught on. They knew all about his dishonest ways. Before long Harry was very unpopular with his immediate coworkers, who knew the boss couldn't see through the smoke screen.

As God's employee, can you imagine going to your heavenly reward and trying to put one over on the one who knows all about you, from your first thought to your last action? He doesn't need a heaven full of dishonest workers any more than a corporation does. So He doesn't start creating them here on earth. While we're here, God begins our heavenly training by creating honest, hardworking people He can be proud of. He should be able to count on our treating our bosses right. After all, aren't we really serving the Ruler of the universe, not the CEO of the company?

Lord, I don't want to be a pretend person.
Help me to treat my boss as well as I treat You.

USEFUL TO GOD

But God chose the foolish things of the world to shame the wise;
God chose the weak things of the world to shame the strong.

1 CORINTHIANS 1:27 NIV

● ● ●

Maybe you aren't in management, or if you are, you may feel as if you're still on a very low rung of the ladder. If you work for people who have a lot of smarts, it's easy to start feeling as if you have nothing of value to offer. After all, aren't these other folks so much better than you?

Be encouraged. God isn't just looking for the really smart, the really gifted, or the really wealthy to do His work. In fact, He seems to prefer to use the quiet, lowly, but obedient person.

You may not reach a high position in your job. Perhaps you'll stay pretty much where you are now for as long as you stay with this company. But whatever your place, if your life honors God, your faith can have a powerful impact on your workplace. People will remember you and recognize the things you stood for. A few may even feel shame and wish they'd followed in your footsteps.

Lord, no matter where You want to use me, I want to
be Your servant. Let my light shine for You today.

GIVE GOD THE CREDIT

"Let the one who boasts boast in the Lord."

1 CORINTHIANS 1:31 NIV

❋ ❋ ❋

Are you on a spiritual high? Is life going well for you in the workplace? Then you may be in a very dangerous place. You may feel tempted to take credit for all the good things. Perhaps you're starting to feel as if you have some special spiritual knowledge that makes you better than others. Or maybe you've reached out to people on the job, they've responded to Jesus, and you're starting to feel as if you're an extraordinary witness for God.

It's great that God is using you so powerfully, but don't forget that He's the one giving you the power to speak those words and that it's His Spirit that's touching the hearts. We are tools in God's hands, and we need to be ready for Him to pick up and use us, but we're not the ones who made the plans and brought them to completion.

Praise God for your successes, but remember that without Him, they are impossible. Boast about what happened, if you want, but boast that Jesus did it, not you.

Lord, I want to lift up Your name so others know what's happening and who caused it. I could never do this on my own.

MADE FOR MORE

I will praise thee; for I am fearfully and wonderfully made:
marvellous are thy works; and that my soul knoweth right well.
My substance was not hid from thee, when I was made in secret,
and curiously wrought in the lowest parts of the earth.

PSALM 139:14–15

* * *

Hate your job every day? Maybe you're in the wrong one. Perhaps you were never physically or emotionally designed to do this kind of work. After all, God created you with a special purpose and gave you the skills to carry out His plan. If you're not fulfilling His purpose, you're in the wrong place.

Don't let this mistake make you decide you're not suited to any work! God designed you to do something and do it well. He gave you abilities and interests He wants you to use to provide for yourself and your family and glorify Him. You just need to *find* the work you're made for.

Explore your interests and discover your strengths. Pray for direction. Then look for the job God made you for. It's out there somewhere. He created a marvelous, incredibly detailed work in you, and He'll help you discover what to do with it.

Thank You, Lord, for creating an amazing me.
Help me use all my abilities as You'd like to have them used.

GOOD ADVICE

And the soldiers likewise demanded of him, saying, And what
shall we do? And he said unto them, Do violence to no man,
neither accuse any falsely; and be content with your wages.

LUKE 3:14

* * *

Kind of odd, isn't it, that soldiers would come to a holy man for work advice? You wouldn't think John the Baptist would have much to say to them. But these men recognized that they could not compartmentalize their lives. There was not one set of rules for work and another for their religious lives.

Most of us are not soldiers, but this advice not to take advantage of others, to be honest, and to live within our wages, not looking for dishonest gain to pad our incomes, still works for us. Whether we have a great deal of authority or just a little, through John, Jesus tells us we should treat others gently, just as we would want them to treat us. Intimidation tactics and false accusations are not for children of God.

Need more work guidance? Today, have you asked God, "What should I do?" Then have you listened to and obeyed His answer?

Show me what I should do today, God,
and help me obey Your commands.

GOD'S PLACE

Then Jesus beholding him loved him, and said unto him,
One thing thou lackest: go thy way, sell whatsoever thou hast,
and give to the poor, and thou shalt have treasure in heaven:
and come, take up the cross, and follow me.

MARK 10:21

❋ ❋ ❋

This young man who came to Jesus had begun to worship things, perhaps things he'd worked hard for, instead of God. So in an ultimately humbling statement, the Master asked the young man to set all his possessions aside and follow Him. Sadly, the man turned Jesus down because he loved things more than he loved God. He was surely on the wrong track: the Bible never speaks of loving anything but God or other people, because love is appropriately given to someone who can respond.

Jesus didn't hate this young man. His heart reached out to him in love. But because He knew things could never replace Himself, He asked the man to set aside all those distractions and turn to Him alone.

Has work become your love? Is it in God's place? You can't stop working, but you can give your work to Him. He'll love you more than any job.

No matter how much I love my work,
let me always love You more, Lord.

GOOD FOR EVIL

Recompense to no man evil for evil.
Provide things honest in the sight of all men.

ROMANS 12:17

* * *

"It's not fair!" We've all wanted to cry that at some point in our careers. No matter how dedicated we are to our work, at some point we'll face a situation where we feel we've been treated unfairly, whether we have to give up a vacation week we really wanted or don't get the job transfer we applied for.

When that happens, how do we react? Do we take it out on the company in subtle ways, not working as hard as we used to or taking home a few "extra" pencils for the kids?

It's a natural response to feel hurt when we don't get something we wanted badly. Our hopes are dashed when something enjoyable falls through. But that doesn't mean we have the right to retaliate. Returning evil for evil just puts more evil in the world. But being aboveboard and honest, even when things don't go our way, will return good to the world.

Lord, I know what unfairness is like, and I hate
to be on its receiving end. But when life is unfair,
help me turn it to Your good as a testimony to right.

THAT EXTRA MILE

"And whoever compels you to go one mile, go with him two."
<small>MATTHEW 5:41 NKJV</small>

❋ ❋ ❋

In our independent society, the idea of going an extra mile is completely foreign—as foreign as the ancient Jews who were forced into the Roman army's service on the whim of these pagan leaders. Faced with the same situation, we'd stand on our rights, rights no Jew in Jesus' age had. Things have surely changed in this world, so does that mean we no longer have to go another mile with someone who forces us to divert our lives to a place we'd rather not go?

No, because this verse is still in the Bible. So when your boss asks you to work an extra hour of overtime, and it takes two instead, maybe you shouldn't gripe. If you get moved off one project and onto another harder one, it doesn't give you complaining rights.

Remember, Jesus went more than an extra mile for us. He set aside His glory, came to earth, and suffered to bring us into heaven with Him. For that, we can go more than an extra couple of miles.

When I'm tempted to complain, Jesus, remind me of the sacrifice You made for me. Then help me do what You've asked with a cheerful attitude.

BLIND EYES

*And [Jesus] was transfigured before them: and his face
did shine as the sun, and his raiment was white as the light.*

MATTHEW 17:2

* * *

Tell your coworkers you're going to church, and what response
will you get? Some may commend you, but others may mock you
because their eyes are shut to who Jesus is.

Those coworkers are a little like the disciples the day before
the transfiguration. Jesus appeared to them, and instead of the
ordinary-looking human who roamed Israel, Peter, James, and
John saw His glory. Though they'd known Jesus for years, the
idea that He was not *just* a person took on a meaning it had not
had the day before.

When we accept Jesus, we, too, have a glimpse of His glory.
We treat Him differently, and our lives change drastically. But
we work with people who haven't yet seen Jesus' glory. Like the
disciples, they don't have a clear picture of who He is. If they did,
they wouldn't treat you—or Him—like that.

When coworkers mock, understand that they are blind. Pray
for them; share as much as you can. And maybe someday, through
your life, they *will* see Jesus.

---

*Lord, give me compassion for those who cannot see You.
Touch their lives and show them who You are.*

AN ATTITUDE ADJUSTMENT

"Suppose one of you wants to build a tower.
Won't you first sit down and estimate the cost to
see if you have enough money to complete it?"

LUKE 14:28 NIV

● ● ●

Sometimes money becomes a job issue when a company is short on cash. As workers, we may complain when we can't easily get supplies that have been plentiful until now. It's natural to complain that our raises weren't larger.

When we do that, we're not seeing things from our employer's point of view. Like the man who prepared to build a tower, the bosses are looking toward the future. They've considered the company's past track record and future prospects, and they may have found their financial cupboard to be bare. So they're taking steps to correct that.

We can carp, condemn, and complain. That won't put extra cash in our bosses' hands. It won't increase sales. But it will hurt our spirits and those around us. So maybe it's time to change our attitudes, pitch in, and help.

Lord, I hate it when money is tight. Help me to understand,
have patience, and depend on You to provide.

"FOOLISH" WISDOM

For since in the wisdom of God the world through its
wisdom did not know him, God was pleased through the
foolishness of what was preached to save those who believe.

1 CORINTHIANS 1:21 NIV

* * *

Speak out about Jesus to enough stubbornly unbelieving coworkers, and you'll quickly get the message that what they believe makes all the sense in the world, and what you are preaching is utterly ridiculous.

Don't give in to a desire to go along with the crowd when you feel frustrated about speaking out for Jesus. Don't ignore the faith in your heart and exchange it for worldly "wisdom." In the end, you'll find that's anything but wise, and it will take you to miserable places God's true wisdom doesn't go.

But God's seemingly foolish wisdom not only brings you a peace-filled life with Jesus on earth; it also offers a heavenly eternal reward. Though your scoffing coworkers may deny your testimony on earth, eventually they will not deny their eternal options. One day, in judgment, God will make their own foolishness plain.

So don't be a pest, but keep on showing them Jesus. Someday, that scoffing may turn to faith because you weren't foolish enough to give up.

Lord, keep me as a faithful testimony to You, wherever I work.

WORKING FOR GOD

Whatever you do, work at it with all your heart,
as working for the Lord, not for human masters.

* * *

Ever wished you were the boss? Perhaps you didn't like the way
your boss handled things and thought you knew a better way. When
you feel like that, do you shut down and become as unhelpful as
possible? Or do you still do your best work, putting your heart into
it and calmly hoping all will work out better than you expected?

However you feel, shutting down is not what God has in mind.
God is your ultimate boss, and He says you need to treat your
boss with respect. Your boss may not have all the answers, but
God placed him in that position, and you are accountable to him.

If your boss's plan doesn't work out, he'll have to report that
to his boss and bear the brunt of the criticism. If you've done your
work poorly, your boss will take the blame. So do your best job,
humbly offer helpful insights, and work as a team. Remember,
you're really reporting to God, and you want His "well done" at
the end of the day.

Lord, help me remember that I'm really working for You.
Let all that I do be pleasing in Your sight.

HEAVENLY "PAYCHECK"

You know that you will receive an inheritance from the Lord as a reward. It is the Lord Christ you are serving.

COLOSSIANS 3:24 NIV

＊ ＊ ＊

You mean I'm going to get a reward for my work—and it isn't just a paycheck?

Yes, absolutely. You didn't think God would ask you to work for Him without giving you something in return, did you? How unlike our generous God that would be!

When we find ourselves in work situations we don't approve of and have a hard time making ourselves do the right thing, we can fix our eyes on God's reward. The fringe benefits may be small. But the benefits of obeying God make up for every lost dollar and difficult situation. Our eyes are on something much larger, a benefit that will not be destroyed by time or decay.

As we serve Jesus in our workday, He promises that we are earning heavenly benefits. Though we may not name them here on earth, we know the God who offers them and trust that our imaginations will pale beside the reality God holds for us in heaven.

From nine to five—or whatever my hours—I want to continue to serve You, Lord. Every moment of every day should reflect Your love in my life.

BIBLICAL MANAGEMENT

Masters, provide your slaves with what is right and fair,
because you know that you also have a Master in heaven.
COLOSSIANS 4:1 NIV

❋ ❋ ❋

Wronging workers—whether you're at the top of the corporate ladder or many rungs down—has its price. It may cause some people to quit, leaving management in a bind; others simply become angry and hard to manage. But that price is small compared to the spiritual one. The job's cost is never worth the spiritual pain.

A cutthroat management attitude is far from a biblical one. And Christians who get caught up in this mentality quickly find their spiritual life suffering. Soon they may be asked to do things they know are wrong. Bound by the need to work, they take steps they'd rather not—and end up feeling guilty.

If your company asks you to do something wrong, stand up for what's right. It may cost you your job, but gain you heaven's reward.

Whoever does work for me should be treated fairly, Lord.
Help me live up to that commitment every day.

LOVE EVEN THEN

But I say unto you which hear, Love your enemies,
do good to them which hate you.

LUKE 6:27

* * *

The love Jesus described here is no easy task. On our own, we could barely even start to do it. Before long, we'd get caught up in resentment and anger. Only God can help us love our enemies to the point where we actually do good for them. He gave us a wonderful example of such love in His Son, Jesus, who died for people who didn't care about Him, detested every word out of His mouth, and couldn't stand a thing about Him. We were some of those people before we came to know Him.

Some of the people we work with may not exactly be enemies, but they may be exasperating. When they expect work in less time than it takes to do it, we could let the resentment burn. Or we could decide that they, too, have pressures on them; and since they don't do our jobs, they can't be realistic about time management. We can love them anyway and do our best. Then we'll be doing good, and God will commend us.

Lord, help me love the people who make me crazy.
I know they often don't do it intentionally.

REST IN GOD

*"My Presence will go with you,
and I will give you rest."*

• • •

Wouldn't you love to have this promise that God gave Moses, to know that when you needed rest, it would be there?

Sometimes we get so caught up in work all week and chores all weekend that rest never becomes part of the picture. But did you notice that Moses never took a vacation? He never found a comfy oasis and settled down for a week or two, though he and his people traveled for forty years in the desert.

How did Moses make it when the pressure was high? Did the Bible forget to tell about the days he simply disappeared for a rest? No, because Moses' rest was in God. Whenever the people were frustrating him, Moses turned to Him in supplication. As he drew close to his Lord in prayer, peace settled over the prophet's soul.

God offers you that peace, too. Just spend some quiet time talking with Him. It can feel more restful than a month's vacation.

*Thank You, Lord, for the peace and rest I find in You.
When the world starts pushing in on me, help me
trust in Your will and follow Your way.*

NO NITPICKING

But woe unto you, Pharisees! for ye tithe mint and rue and all
manner of herbs, and pass over judgment and the love of God:
these ought ye to have done, and not to leave the other undone.

LUKE 11:42

＊　＊　＊

As Christians, we may know all the "rules." Those rules aren't
entirely bad. Avoiding questionable things is good, if it doesn't
become a "god" in itself. But the Pharisees got so caught up in
their legalistic rule keeping, they pushed aside things that were
really important to God—they lost track of God's character. They
turned a loving God into simply a nitpicky idol, ready to object
to any unkept rule.

We, too, can become class-A nitpickers. If we work with
someone from another denomination, we can get so caught up
in our doctrinal differences that we ruin our testimonies. If our
coworkers see nothing but disagreement, they will never be drawn
to any church. But if they see love, our Lord will become appealing.

Don't nitpick over every herb in your garden and forget to
show God's justice and love—because then you'll be no better than
Jesus' enemies, the Pharisees.

Lord, I want to shine brightly with Your love,
not with legalism. Fill me with Your Spirit now.

AMAZING LOVE

The Father loveth the Son, and hath given all things into
his hand. He that believeth on the Son hath everlasting life:
and he that believeth not the Son shall not see life;
but the wrath of God abideth on him.

* * *

In salvation, we became inextricably bound to the love of the
Godhead. We can't fathom how God did it or why. Why us and
not others? If we're honest, we know we didn't have anything that
made us so special that we deserved eternity.

So why did God choose you and maybe not the coworker next
to you? He alone knows. Be glad that He loves you. But don't let it
end there. Share the love of Jesus with others around you. Maybe
you're not good at preaching, but you can show what God is like
by being honest. You can show His caring by lending an ear to a
coworker who's going through a personal crisis. You can offer your
apartment-dwelling coworker some tomatoes from your garden
when you have a bumper crop.

You may never hear that person pray to receive Him, but your
coworker just may have felt the first touch of Jesus' love.

Use me, Lord, wherever You want to.
Show me how to share Your love today.

NO SUCH THING AS PERFECT

For therefore we both labour and suffer reproach,
because we trust in the living God, who is the
Saviour of all men, specially of those that believe.

1 TIMOTHY 4:10

❋ ❋ ❋

When you feel persecuted at work, it's easy to wish that you could share your nine-to-five time with only believers. *How wonderful,* it's tempting to think, *if everyone I worked with was a Christian. There would be no arguments, no problems!*

If you worked solely in the company of Christians, you'd soon discover that they're people just like anyone else. They have different points of view and differences of opinion. Just knowing God doesn't solve every problem.

The apostle Paul knew that. The reproach he talks about in this verse was not only from unbelievers—he also had plenty of trouble from the churches he ministered to.

Whether you work with lots of Christians or are the only one, when work becomes hard and your faith is an issue, take Paul as your example and stand firm. God doesn't promise perfect workplaces, just a relationship with the Perfect One.

Lord, the workplace will never be perfect,
but thank You that I can still work for the perfect God.

A TEAM EFFORT

I planted the seed, Apollos watered it,
but God has been making it grow.

1 CORINTHIANS 3:6 NIV

* * *

Did you know you are part of a team—with God? It's true! You're part of a squad to bring His good news to a hurting world.

Paul was part of a team, too. He came to Corinth and preached the Gospel. A man named Apollos helped these new Christians grow. But it wasn't long before Corinthian Christians started dividing up according to which leader they thought was best. Some boasted of their connection with Paul, while others claimed that being ministered to by Apollos was better. Paul pointed out that God caused spiritual growth, no matter who did the preaching.

Whether it's in church or the workplace, no one gets results alone—everything's a team effort, no matter what your task is. So recognize the input others have. Treat your coworkers as a team and help that team to work at its peak efficiency.

You may have had an idea, but others created it, advertised it, and took it out to the marketplace. Recognize your place in the team and give thanks for those who help you—God especially!

Let me be humble enough, Lord, to recognize
the others on my team and be thankful for them.

INDEBTED

Let no debt remain outstanding, except the continuing debt to
love one another, for whoever loves others has fulfilled the law.
ROMANS 13:8 NIV

* * *

On your first job or a new one, someone probably helped you learn
the ropes. As your career has gone on, people have assisted you
in other ways—the new staff person has given you a hand when
you were overloaded with work, or your boss has taken up some
slack for you.

Whether or not you feel like admitting it, you are in their debt.
But they've already been paid by the company, so what could you do
about it? Lots. You may not pay back your boss today, but someday
he'll need help. Maybe you can help train a new employee. Your new
coworker may need help on how to handle a situation. Or maybe
you can offer to double-check something for her.

When you can't repay a debt, you can show your love for the
other person by lending a hand. And if you can't give that help
to the person who helped you, pass it on to another coworker. If
everyone does that, your company will be a great place to work.

Lord, when someone helps me, let me repay the
debt with love. I want to work in a great place.

HUMAN CONNECTIONS

Rejoice with them that do rejoice,
and weep with them that weep.

ROMANS 12:15

* * *

Shortly after Sheila began to work for Marvin, he told her that emotions had no place in the workplace. He expected his staff to follow a strict professional code in which no one shared any personal situations. Sheila wasn't surprised that people didn't last long in the department. It wasn't long before she was considering a job change herself.

When you're on the job, you shouldn't spend much time on your personal situation. You're there to work, not solve personal problems or improve your home life. But the wise company will also allow people to share a few personal joys and sorrows. People, after all, are people. They don't drop their humanity at the door of the workplace.

Be careful not to shortchange your boss. Don't spend hours chatting with coworkers. But when someone shares about her new niece, congratulate her. When another's son missed making the team, let him know you're sorry.

When people rejoice with those who are happy and hurt for the sorrowful, they work better together. A team cares about what's on the heart of each member. So care for your team.

Lord, I want to share others' joys and sorrows.
Help me do it in the right way.

RAT RACE

Be kindly affectioned one to another with
brotherly love; in honour preferring one another.

ROMANS 12:10

✳ ✳ ✳

Competition can keep you on your toes—or it can kill an office environment. How you deal with it makes all the difference. In some companies, it's everyone for himself—or herself! The urge to get to the top surpasses everything else, and a cutthroat attitude kills any team spirit that tries to develop. Other companies learn to foster friendly competition that helps workers do their best without destroying interworker connections.

This verse was addressed to the church. Paul didn't want the Romans putting themselves first and becoming puffed up in their own conceit. But the truth Paul wrote also works on the job. You may not always agree with your coworkers' attitudes or actions, but treat them with love and respect. Give them credit for their good work, and help them when you can. That's the way to "get ahead" and honor God at the same time. If your work environment demands that you do anything else, maybe it's time for a new, God-honoring career.

Getting ahead at any price can be dangerous, Lord.
Help me honor You at every point in my career.

ENCOURAGING WORDS

"Now go out and encourage your men. I swear by the Lord
that if you don't go out, not a man will be left with you by
nightfall. This will be worse for you than all the calamities
that have come on you from your youth till now."

2 SAMUEL 19:7 NIV

❋ ❋ ❋

King David learned the wisdom of putting aside his own troubles
and encouraging the men who fought for him when he heard this
warning from his commander, Joab. Caught up with mourning the
death of his favorite son, David ignored the men who had saved
him and his family from certain destruction. When Joab warned
that the soldiers felt unappreciated by the king they had saved,
David spoke the appropriate words.

Does someone work for you? Then it's a wise decision to offer
honest words of praise. Unencouraged people are not motivated
to work hard; all of us like appreciation. Working for a long time
without a "thanks" or "well done" turns every job into a chore.

As a boss, you may not always feel like giving appreciation,
but do it anyway. Make sure the "warriors" on your team get the
encouragement they deserve, or you may find yourself with no
one to "rule"!

Lord, help me say words of encouragement
that my workers or coworkers need to hear.

BUILDING WHAT COUNTS

And they said, Go to, let us build us a city and a tower,
whose top may reach unto heaven; and let us make us a name,
lest we be scattered abroad upon the face of the whole earth.

GENESIS 11:4

* * *

What are you building with your life—a reputation, an ability to help others, a name for faithfulness? Or are you building a career that will make your name?

The people of Babel were building their own name and future on their own terms. They wanted the world to know them, and for many centuries it did. But the Tower of Babel and the city were finally destroyed. The people who wanted to be engraved on others' memories became part of history.

Our careers easily become part of history, too. A few years from now, no matter how much we do for our companies, we may fall into the back of others' memories.

We can seek to become important to other people, or we can seek to be important to God. To do that, we build up His name, not our own; we try to build His kingdom instead of our own reputation. Which are you building today?

Lord, I want Your name to be greater than mine.
Help me build Your kingdom, not my own.

STRUGGLE-LESS?

I want you to know how great a struggle I have for you. . .
[For my hope is] that their hearts may be encouraged.
COLOSSIANS 2:1-2 AMP

❋ ❋ ❋

"Faithful Christians should never suffer." Has anyone ever said words like those to you? They imply that anyone who really knows Jesus has a flawless life. Any troubles encountered are easily overcome.

Those who say such things have never looked at the life of Paul. Who could have been more faithful? Yet he suffered "on the job" from Christians who would not listen to his teachings, persecution from unbelievers, and the struggles that went with his constant travel as he preached the Gospel to the world.

It happens on your job, too. You're working hard and expect that things should go smoothly, but an irritating problem remains. No matter what you do, it's still there. You feel like Paul, who was doing good and getting bad in return.

Look at the problem. See if you are causing it, and fix anything that's wrong. Pray about it. Do whatever God leads you to do. But don't assume that every struggle results from a spiritual flaw. Don't let how much you've suffered determine your success.

Today, does any Christian think Paul's a failure?

Lord, when I face struggles, I want to face them with You.

GROUNDED SELF-ESTEEM

For I say, through the grace given unto me, to every man
that is among you, not to think of himself more highly
than he ought to think; but to think soberly, according
as God hath dealt to every man the measure of faith.

ROMANS 12:3

❋ ❋ ❋

You do a good job, and you're proud of your skills and your work. Maybe you've been complimented on your abilities. Great! But are you getting a swollen head from it?

Whether you're a big fish in a small pond or a small fish in a big pond, beware of letting praise or compliments make your head the size of a weather balloon. Remember, you'll never do everything perfectly. Remind yourself, too, that other people have skills and abilities that you lack, and having them as your partners in the workplace makes a company run smoothly.

Occasionally, we all are tempted to decide we're terrific. That's okay, as long as we keep our self-opinion in perspective. It's nice to feel good about ourselves sometimes, if we treat others respectfully and appreciate their abilities as well. So today compliment someone else on a job well done. After all, you aren't the only one who needs appreciation.

Lord, help me to see myself as You see me—in a balanced way.

CREATIVE POWER

God. . .gives life to the dead and calls those
things which do not exist as though they did.

ROMANS 4:17 NKJV

❊ ❊ ❊

When you work, you use tools to create something. Without a computer, pens, pencils, or other equipment, you couldn't get very far on the job. From the beginning of time, people needed fire and clay to create pots, plows or sticks to turn up the earth, and sheep to use for clothes and food.

But God creates *ex nihilo*—"out of nothing." He didn't have to have something to create another thing. Out of nothing He made the earth and heavens. Rivers began to flow and stars to twinkle in a night sky, formed from the mind of God alone.

Humans can be incredibly creative, using artistic talent, a bent for words, or physical skills that allow them to make furniture, homes, and equipment. But none of us can create with just a thought. As you work today, give thanks to the one who gave you a computer and the other items you need. Appreciate all He has done for you, and be amazed at the awesome creativity of the Creator.

Thank You, Lord, for creating me and giving
me the abilities I need to work. I praise You
for Your wonderful imagination and love.

OUR PROTECTION

For I heard many mocking: "Fear on every side!" "Report," they say, "and we will report it!" All my acquaintances watched for my stumbling, saying, "Perhaps he can be induced; then we will prevail against him, and we will take our revenge on him."

JEREMIAH 20:10 NKJV

✿ ✿ ✿

No matter what you do, there are times when you'll get someone's back up. Maybe it's a coworker who's jealous that you got your last raise when she got none. Or perhaps it's someone who had an idea that you critiqued in the line of work, and he'll never let you forget it.

Jeremiah knew what that was like. He'd been a good prophet, but what he did was not popular, and it got him into big trouble. Even his friends were against him. On the one hand, Jeremiah felt that compulsion from God to preach, but preaching had become dangerous.

Work isn't always a "safe place." We put ourselves on the line every day in many minor ways. But no matter who goes against us, like Jeremiah, we can trust in God as our protector. When we follow His will, even the most dangerous place will be safe.

*Thank You, Jesus, for protecting me on the job.
When I'm there, like Jeremiah, I want to be faithful.*

IT CAN'T BE EARNED

Now to the one who works, wages are not credited as
a gift but as an obligation. However, to the one who
does not work but trusts God who justifies the ungodly,
their faith is credited as righteousness.

ROMANS 4:4-5 NIV

❀ ❀ ❀

You probably don't work for free—you need money to live on, pay the rent with, and save for a rainy day.

Though the Bible recognizes the need to earn a living, it also tells us God's kingdom isn't like that. We can't work our way into heaven because we can't do anything to make ourselves right with God. The only one who can do that is God's perfect Son, Jesus. When we believe that He died in order to forgive our sins, our eternal destination becomes heaven. God gives us that gift for doing nothing more than trusting in Him.

So today, instead of spending time catching up on office work after hours, why not trust in God? Spend time in worship, not work; and instead of trying to enter heaven on your own credit, you'll arrive there safely on your trust in Jesus.

Thank You, Lord, that I can only enter into heaven by
trust in You. I could work 24-7 and never build
up the righteousness You offer as a gift.

BOLD TO OVERCOME

And Caleb stilled the people before Moses,
and said, Let us go up at once, and possess it;
for we are well able to overcome it.

NUMBERS 13:30

❀　❀　❀

Caleb didn't go with the popular vote when asked about the people who inhabited the promised land. When most of the other spies who'd gone in to scope out Canaan said the people living there were too powerful to overcome, this faithful man resisted the idea. In the back of his mind was surely the idea that God had brought them this far, and He would never desert them. They could certainly conquer in His power.

On the job, you may feel as discouraged as the worrying Israelites. The work looks so hard, and the obstacles seem large. When they appear that way, are you seeing with faithful eyes like Caleb's, which saw *everything* as being small compared to God? Probably not.

God has brought you this far, and He'll never let you down. But it's up to you to trust in Him. If you do, you can have all the success He has in store for you—spiritually and in the workplace.

Lord, I don't know if I can be as faithful as Caleb, but my heart
wants to. Help me trust You to overcome every obstacle.

HARD TO RESIST

For the good that I would I do not:
but the evil which I would not, that I do.
ROMANS 7:19

* * *

You want to do a good job. You're committed to doing well and building a good career. But something just grabs ahold of you. You know it's wrong. God would never approve; still, you start heading in the wrong direction.

Though we know God and want to serve Him wholeheartedly, at times that old sin nature sticks its head up and seems to commandeer our lives. We struggle to resist, and sometimes we aren't fully successful. Occasionally, we don't even want to oppose sin. The apostle Paul knew what that was like. He knew full well what the right thing was, yet he balked at doing it. Something inside drew even this spiritual giant back to the wrong way.

As we grow in Jesus, temptations may lessen, but they'll always hang around at the fringes of our spirits. Every day we need to alertly guard against evil desires. When one tugs at our souls, we must rush to God and cling to Him for aid. No sin situation is hopeless: in Him, we *can* still do right.

Lord, I need Your help to stand firm. In Your Spirit
I can resist evil, so fill me with Your strength today.

MAKE THINGS RIGHT

"And if I say to a wicked person, 'You will surely die,'
but they then turn away from their sin and do what is just
and right...that person will surely live; they will not die."

EZEKIEL 33:14–15 NIV

* * *

Have you ever made a mistake on the job? How did your boss treat it? Chances are that if you immediately took steps to clean up your act, you stayed with the company. You showed you cared, and your boss cut you some slack.

It's the same with God. He isn't a pushover who never punishes sin. But neither will He hold sin against someone who recognizes his wrongdoing and turns from it, faithfully trying to make right the wrong he's done and showing his change of heart by obeying God's commands. What point would there be in God punishing a person who was no longer wicked? It would go against everything in His Word. When we do what He asks and follow His law, God forgives. No matter how bad that wickedness was, it's gone forever.

God offers to clean each of our slates today. We only have to ask Him to use the eraser on our lives.

Forgive me, Lord, for my sins. I want to make
them right, when possible, and follow Your decrees.

WHO'S IN CHARGE?

"Even from eternity I am He, and there is none who can deliver out of My hand; I act and who can reverse it?"

ISAIAH 43:13 NASB

* * *

Who's in charge here? you may wonder when work gets crazy. When your job seems confusing, life appears to be out of control.

Maybe your company has made some poor choices. You may be heading in the wrong direction in your personal life. But none of it is so crazy or disorganized that God is unaware of it and can't deliver it. Nor has God forgotten you, your coworkers, or your family. He's in control when life is normal or not so normal.

Others may declare that God made the world then forgot it. Or they may say there is no God or that He can't or won't do a thing to help you. You know better. Just as the Israelites who worshipped idols had lost out on God's power, your coworkers or friends who don't know Him can't appreciate what He's really like. They don't appreciate His ability to save both your soul and life situations.

When God has you in His hand, He's in control of your life, no matter what happens to the rest of the world.

Thank You, Lord, for being in control of my life.

MESSAGE BEARERS

" 'Then they will know that I am the LORD, when I
have made the land a desolate waste because
of all the detestable things they have done.' "

EZEKIEL 33:29 NIV

❀ ❀ ❀

Sin creates desolate lives. Finding the damage sin does to our personal worlds doesn't require a microscope. Signs appear in a coworker's divorce or the career-minded selfishness of one person who ruins an efficient team. We know the desolation sin created in our lives when we failed to walk with God.

Though we might like to, we can't control the sin in other people's lives. No matter how much we encourage coworkers to make right choices, think of others, and turn to God, we cannot make them choose wisely. We can only bear the message, letting them know how sin destroys relationships and ruins happiness. We do that by sharing examples of how sin hurt our lives and showing blessings God has given as we've followed Him. Through our personal testimony and the way we live each day for God, we can fight back against the wasteland. Like Ezekiel, we may not always find our message welcome, but it's one that needs to be told with kindness, gentleness, and care.

Lord, use my life to turn people away
from sin and toward life in You.

WORDS TO LIVE BY

"My people. . .hear your words, but they do not put them into practice. Their mouths speak of love, but their hearts are greedy for unjust gain. Indeed, to them you are nothing more than one who sings love songs with a beautiful voice."

EZEKIEL 33:31–32 NIV

* * *

Are you a Christian who claims to love God but never acts on that concept? Then the Bible compares your faith to entertainment, not commitment.

People you work with can tell which you are. They can identify the "entertainment Christians," who are in it just for the fun, from the ones who really mean it. Maybe unbelievers don't give less serious Christians as much grief as the committed ones, but they know which ones mean what they say. And when they need to know about God, to whom do you think they go?

Are you listening to God's Word but not living by it? Then maybe, like the people in these verses, something other than God is first in your heart. You're listening to Him and treating Him as a singer with a lovely voice instead of the omnipotent Holy One who has words of life you can live by.

Oh omnipotent Holy One, I don't want to entertain but show commitment. Help me live for You.

UNSPOKEN PRAYERS

Now to him who is able to do immeasurably more than all
we ask or imagine, according to his power that is at work
within us, to him be glory in the church and in Christ Jesus
throughout all generations, for ever and ever! Amen.

EPHESIANS 3:20–21 NIV

❀　❀　❀

Have you ever had God answer a prayer you hadn't even gotten around to praying yet? Maybe your mind was on a problem at work or a coworker's troubles. You mulled it over, but by the time you got to formal prayer, it had slipped off into mental oblivion.

Then you went to the office one morning and learned that God had been at work all along and solved the problem you'd shelved. The situation came to a beautiful conclusion, without your having prayed at all. How awful you felt that you'd never even brought it before the Savior!

None of us should ignore prayer, and it's a good idea to keep a prayer list handy; but even when we fail, God doesn't. We may ponder something without prayer, yet in His grace He answers even that unspoken need. How much He deserves our praise!

I praise You, Lord, for doing more than I'd
even think of asking for. I give You all the glory.

HOW UNIQUE!

[Deborah] held court under the Palm of Deborah. . .and the
Israelites went up to her to have their disputes decided.

* * *

What an unusual person Deborah was! Judges were usually men, yet she held this position of importance, deciding major issues for the people of Israel. In a time when most people thought of women as being fairly unimportant, she held a powerful position.

Like Deborah, we can find ourselves in unusual jobs. Perhaps you're the only person of your sex on your job. Maybe you are young, working with people greatly senior to you. Or perhaps you are the only person of your race on the job. Being the one who's different can be a challenge. Your position can be one to complain about or one to learn from. The scriptures don't show Deborah whining or complaining. She took charge of the situation. She did her best for God, and an impressive best it was.

Whether you fit in completely or find yourself in a tough spot, you're there to serve God, not complain or quit easily. So make even your differences work for God, no matter what they are.

I may feel different, Lord, but You've given me this place.
Let me serve You by doing my best every day.

HELP LIKE RAIN

*Ask the LORD for rain in the spring, for he makes
the storm clouds. And he will send showers of
rain so every field becomes a lush pasture.*

ZECHARIAH 10:1 NLT

* * *

By and large, we're no longer an agrarian culture, so the meaning of this passage loses something in the cultural translation. If there's a drought, we may pay more for our vegetables, but we don't fear for our lives.

The small farmer of the Old Testament period didn't have that luxury. No rain, no crops, no life. Asking God for rain was no unimportant matter. Yet the people of Judah had ignored God's ability to provide their need. Instead they turned to idols, expecting them to give an "easy out" without expecting the obedience Judah refused God.

We still need God's providence, even if we don't work in a field and harvest its fruits. He's the one who provides us with our jobs, our homes, and our daily food. So when we face problems on the job or need money to pay our bills, we can turn to Him and ask for the rain of His wisdom. It provides for us as surely as the wet stuff from the clouds waters the fields.

*Lord, I need Your help in so many ways.
Send Your rain on every portion of my life.*

SLACKING OFF

One who is slack in his work is brother to one who destroys.
PROVERBS 18:9 NIV

❀　❀　❀

If you've slacked off at work, have you thought of yourself as being destructive? Probably not. But ask the person who had to take up that slack if it destroyed his opinion of you.

If you weren't up to speed because of a temporary circumstance, perhaps your coworker didn't think that harshly of you. Perhaps you even found some ways to make it up to your coworker.

But the person who habitually slacks off causes real problems in the office or factory. People resent someone who habitually won't pull her weight. For a while she can get away with it, but eventually the boss begins to see the effects of that slackness, and she moves on, either fired or demoted to a job where she won't do much harm.

More than that, working hard isn't just something Mom and Dad told you to do so you could earn the big bucks. It's an attitude God designed you to have. So don't slack off—work to please the one who created you to honor Him, from nine-to-five or at any other hour.

Lord, I want to build up, not destroy.
Keep me working faithfully for You.

WISE WORDS

The mouths of fools are their undoing,
and their lips are a snare to their very lives.

PROVERBS 18:7 NIV

* * *

"I never should have opened my mouth," Kate lamented. "It was a foolish thing to tell Sam about our boss's plans, even though they weren't confidential. If I'd known it'd backfire on me like this, I never would have said a word." Kate knew what she'd done was unwise; unfortunately, she hadn't realized that before she spoke.

Thinking before we speak is a wise workplace decision. We need to weigh the impact of our words, what response the person we're talking to may have, and other issues specific to our workplaces. We don't want to tell a confidence to the biggest gossip in the company, even if she is so nice. Nor do we want to hurt the feelings of someone who is particularly sensitive on a subject.

Unwise words may show we are not living in God's wisdom but our own sin; or even if we are not doing wrong, they can land us in impossible situations. Taking this practical advice from God's Word and thinking before we speak saves us a lot of trouble and heartache.

Lord, I want to speak wisely and keep my soul clean.
Keep me from doing wrong with my words.

PRAYER'S POWER

But we will give ourselves continually to prayer,
and to the ministry of the word.

ACTS 6:4

❀ ❀ ❀

The apostles recognized prayer as an element critical to their work of spreading the Gospel. Without God's guidance and blessing, the work could not be accomplished.

Though we may not preach to multitudes, prayer is important in our lives, too. With it we can do our jobs better and lift up coworkers who are under stress or have personal problems. We can even pray for the decisions our bosses have to make so that they will make wise choices.

Many non-Christians don't think of prayer as "practical." They see it as some airy thing that doesn't get the job done and wonder why Christians even bother with it. Sometimes, though, those who doubt prayer's power have a real crisis, like an illness or financial trouble. Then it's amazing how open they can be to the words "I'll pray for you." So offer to lift those unbelievers up in prayer, both for their own salvation and for the need at hand.

Remember, the work does not go on without prayer.

Today, Lord, I know some coworkers who need prayer.
Even if they do not want to know You, I know You
soften hearts. Turn them to You through this situation.

SWEET-SMELLING ACTIONS

*Dead flies putrefy the perfumer's ointment,
and cause it to give off a foul odor; so does a little
folly to one respected for wisdom and honor.*

ECCLESIASTES 10:1 NKJV

* * *

Flies were just a way of life in ancient Israel. No refrigeration, few preservatives—you had to expect something like this to happen. Stinky things were a nasty part of life. Sometimes even in modern life we have to put up with powerful, nasty smells.

But do our lives stink? Whether they do depends on how we act. A little dishonesty or selfishness, and actions that once smelled like perfume instead smell like dead flies.

Some of today's corporate leaders have begun to smell like defunct flies. Their greed has impacted the lives of hundreds— even thousands—of employees and investors who have lost their jobs and money while the leaders lied about their companies' bottom line.

Not only do actions like that stink to us, they stink to God. Those who are found out lose the respect of others and pay a price. It may not consist of jail or unemployment, but it will certainly involve God's disapproval and punishment. Imagine smelling like putrefying flies to God's nose! What could be worse?

*Lord, I want wisdom and honor to be in
my path, not folly. Help me follow You.*

CONSISTENT SPEECH

Laying aside all malice, all deceit,
hypocrisy, envy, and all evil speaking.
1 PETER 2:1 NKJV

❋ ❋ ❋

Certain attitudes, actions, and ways of thinking are not compatible with Christianity. The apostle Peter was absolutely clear on that subject. Though he spoke to the church, and this would be particularly true between fellow believers, it's also true that Christians on the job need to avoid these negatives that usually show up on their tongues.

As a Christian, don't speak one way at work and another way at church. To do so shows a lack of consistency of faith. It's as if you are saying that Jesus' truths are only sometimes valid.

You can't be malicious on Friday then experience a personality change over the weekend. After all, part of the reason God has you on earth on all seven days of the week is to be a testimony—a good testimony—to Him. A malicious comment, a web of deceit, hypocritical or envious attitudes, or nasty words attract no one to Jesus. Instead, people will be more likely to conclude that you've been serving the evil one.

So lay aside all these things. You'll be blessed without them.

Lord, keep my tongue clean and
consistent as a testimony for You.

A GOD TO DEPEND ON

But now they that are younger than I have
me in derision, whose fathers I would have
disdained to have set with the dogs of my flock.

JOB 30:1

❋ ❋ ❋

In today's marketplace, experience often isn't much valued. Kate found out how true that was when she got laid off. Her manager's youthful boss felt anyone who'd been on a job for more than a few years was "deadwood." It didn't make any difference that knowing the clients' past history made selling to them a lot easier. For some time, she struggled with negative feelings about that boss. It hurt to know she'd been judged so unfairly.

Sometimes we don't work with insightful people. Young or old, they may not respect our work or our value to the company. Though they hold a high position, they do not value God's wisdom. These may not be the people we'd prefer to have around us—or prefer to have leading our company. But they hold that position of authority.

No matter what kind of person you work for, that person alone is not in control of your future. Like Job, you depend on God.

Lord, let me focus on the fact that You are ultimately in
control of any manager or boss who touches my career.

MOVING ON

*In the days when the judges ruled. . .there was a famine in the
land. And a certain man of Bethlehem [Elimelech]. . .went to
dwell in the country of Moab, he and his wife and his two sons.*

RUTH 1:1 NKJV

* * *

We don't control what goes on in the world. So when things change
in the marketplace or the economy takes a downturn, we may have
to move to a new location. As we make the move, we leave part of
ourselves in our old home.

Elimelech trudged all the way to Moab with his family to
avoid a famine. They settled down, and his sons married women
from that country. Life was probably pretty good. But Elimelech's
household never forgot the place they came from; Bethlehem
still looked best when trouble came.

We, too, never forget the places we live. Each has a special
memory. No matter where we go, if God is leading us, a special
piece of our heart remains there. When God gives a place to us,
it's forever in our hearts.

*Lord, I only want to live in the places You have set for me.
Wherever I go, let me be "at home" in You.*

KEEP WATCH

Watch therefore: for ye know not
what hour your Lord doth come.

* * *

You may not know what time you'll get to work if you run into frequent traffic jams. You leave early and do your best to get to the office on time, but if a truck's overturned along your route or an accident is blocking the way, you'll get there when you get there.

People are marvelous beings, made by God to do amazing things. But for all our gifts and graces, we still don't know everything—and this side of heaven, we never will.

If we can't be sure when we'll get to work, how could we possibly have an inkling of when Jesus will return? He told us none but the Father will know (Matthew 24:36), yet many people continue guessing or developing elaborate methods for figuring it out. These disobedient ones have missed the point—God expects them to live every day as if He could appear. Always ready, faithful believers put their trust in Him, knowing that what day He comes won't matter if they've been following Him consistently.

The day doesn't matter, but our faith does. Are you ready now?

Lord, each day I want my service to be worthy of You.

NO FREE PASS

" 'Should you then seek great things for yourself? Do not seek them. For I will bring disaster on all people, declares the LORD, but wherever you go I will let you escape with your life.' "

JEREMIAH 45:5 NIV

❀ ❀ ❀

God, who sees all people as equal, refused to reward Baruch's faithfulness to his master, Jeremiah, with good things while the rest of the nation suffered. What Judah endured, the prophet and his companion would experience, too, so no one could accuse God of favoritism. God promised only to spare the scribe's life.

When the company we work for suffers, we suffer. Anything else would be wrong. When corporate officers drain their company while the average worker's pension is destroyed, a scandal ensues. Everyone recognizes that it's wrong for one to benefit mightily while others lose their jobs, their futures, and their investments.

If your company is suffering, do what you can to help. Don't expect to escape just because you're a Christian or a good worker. God doesn't treat people preferentially like that.

Lord, it's hard to suffer, but I don't want Your name to be disgraced. So if I need to live through hard times, be close by my side. With You I can withstand anything.

SO FRUSTRATING!

And Joshua the son of Nun, and Caleb the son of Jephunneh,
which were of them that searched the land, rent their clothes.
NUMBERS 14:6

❋ ❋ ❋

Have you ever felt like Joshua and Caleb? You did your best on
the job and knew just what you were talking about when you gave
your coworkers the information they needed to do the work. To
you, it looked really good, but your bosses didn't believe you and
shot the idea down. It's enough to make anyone tear their clothes
in anguish!

Joshua and Caleb knew how it felt. The only faithful spies into
the promised land, they could see the good God had planned for His
people. But the doubt of the other ten spies ended their "project"
in a few minutes flat. The people didn't believe the honest report
of these two men but went with the bad report of the majority.

When you're not believed, you can be gracious about it.
Give your bosses the benefit of the doubt; after all, unlike Joshua
and Caleb, you do not have biblical testimony to your rightness
on this subject. Accept it without bearing a grudge. That's the
Christian response.

Lord, sometimes I get frustrated enough to tear my clothes.
Keep me well clothed in spirit and even-tempered, too.

KEEP UP THE GOOD WORK

*"I have been very zealous for the LORD God of hosts;
for the children of Israel have forsaken Your covenant,
torn down Your altars, and killed Your prophets with the
sword. I alone am left; and they seek to take my life."*

1 KINGS 19:10 NKJV

❋ ❋ ❋

When he reported to God on the work he'd done, Elijah could say he'd done a good job. In fact, he'd done so well that he'd offended the queen, endangering his life.

At some point, we all have to give an accounting for our work, whether it's at raise time or a project evaluation. Having that responsibility may not seem welcome, but it's a good idea. Accountability keeps us from becoming too caught up in ourselves and reminds us we have a responsibility to our bosses and the company.

Sometimes our skillfulness may even get us in trouble. We may seem to threaten our manager if he thinks we want to take his job. Or we may get that raise someone else wanted. We still need to do our best, without slacking off. After all, like Elijah, we are still accountable to the one we really work for—God.

*Lord, help me do my best for You. Then I can trust that
whatever happens to my career, it will work to Your glory.*

NO-LONGER-IMPOSSIBLE TASKS

*So the wall was finished on the twenty-fifth [day] of [the month]
Elul, in fifty-two days. When all our enemies heard about it,
and all the [Gentile] nations around us saw it, they lost
their confidence; for they recognized that this work had
been accomplished with the help of our God.*

Nehemiah 6:15–16 amp

* * *

Under Nehemiah's leadership, the people of Judah had rebuilt
Jerusalem's wall in record time. Though half the workers had to
stand by fully armed to fend off attack, they'd accomplished their
mission.

The nations around Judah didn't like it one bit. But it wasn't
because of something powerful about the people of Judah—no,
they feared this nation because it was clear God had helped them.

Do you face an impossible task today? Perhaps you need to
get some work done before the end of the day, and you don't see
how you'll do it. Start by asking God's help, then work as hard as
you can, giving your best to your boss. When it's all done, give
God the praise in a tactful way. Perhaps you only need to say, "That
was an answer to prayer," but somehow let the message that God
was with you be known.

*Thank You, Lord, for helping me with impossible tasks.
To You, nothing is impossible.*

A NEED FOR COMPASSION

I pray you, let us leave off this usury. Restore. . .to them,
even this day, their lands, their vineyards, their oliveyards,
and their houses, also the hundredth part of the money,
and of the corn, the wine, and the oil, that ye exact of them.

NEHEMIAH 5:10–11

❀ ❀ ❀

Can you imagine losing your farm and house to those you owe money—even selling yourself into slavery to pay your debts? That's what happened to Nehemiah's people. Hard times fell on Jerusalem, and wealthy Israelites were bringing poor ones down to slavery. The needy borrowed from the well-to-do and soon lost their lands and homes.

A "well, that's business" attitude when it comes to money is not God's approach. He never places cash, checks, or investments above people's lives. And He knows when a lender is charging too much—He calls it usury.

If you are involved in a money-related business, take Nehemiah's words to heart. Bring compassion to your work. But no matter what kind of job you do, there will be times for compassion. Don't stand on your rights, but do what *is* right. God will bless you greatly if you do.

Lord, help me be compassionate in my work.
Teach me to follow Your way.

WITHOUT LOVE. . .

Though I speak with the tongues of men and of angels, and have not charity, I am become as sounding brass, or a tinkling cymbal.

1 CORINTHIANS 13:1

* * *

You may be the most talented person in your company at your job description, but if you aren't gracious, too, you may just seem like noise to the people around you. Who can stand someone who toots his own horn (or clangs her own cymbal) so much that others can't wait to get away from the sound?

Obnoxiousness isn't part of a Christian's job description. The hallmarks of faith are graciousness and love (or charity, as this version calls it). So when you do well in your work, thank God for the gifts He's given you that allow you to serve Him well. Be grateful for the particular gifts of others who work with you.

No matter how gifted you are spiritually or skills-wise, no one appreciates someone who's so full of himself that there's no room for God or anyone else. So have some charity on your job, and you won't just be noise—you'll shed the light of Jesus' love.

Lord, thank You for the abilities that allow me to do my job well. I know they come from You, and I want to avoid pride.

AN IDOL JOB

It is used as fuel for burning; some of it he takes and warms himself, he kindles a fire and bakes bread. But he also fashions a god and worships it; he makes an idol and bows down to it.

ISAIAH 44:15 NIV

❀ ❀ ❀

The Romans not only imagined the well-known grain goddess Demeter, but horticultural gods like Messor, god of mowing, and Sterculius, god of manure. Can you conceive of having a god of manure?

Centuries before the Romans imagined these idols, Isaiah pointed out any god's foolishness. The same tree, he told the Israelites, that creates an idol makes firewood that bakes bread. Just as you wouldn't expect your hearth fire to save you from sin, you can't expect a wooden idol to help you. And it doesn't make any difference if your idol is metal or stone. No created material saves you from sin.

Today, we think of ourselves as sophisticated. We wouldn't bow down to metal, stone, or wood. But idols don't have to be formed from physical materials. A job that keeps you from worship or family time can be as much an idol as anything the Romans forged or carved.

Anything that separates us from God is an idol. Is there one in your life?

Lord, rid my life of idolatry. I want to serve You alone.

YOUNG ≠ UNIMPORTANT

Let no man despise thy youth; but be thou an
example of the believers, in word, in conversation,
in charity, in spirit, in faith, in purity.

1 TIMOTHY 4:12

❋ ❋ ❋

Timothy was young, but he had leadership credentials. He'd grown up with a Christian mother, and he had experienced God's forgiveness for many years. But while he tried to minister to the church in Ephesus, he ran into trouble. He felt funny giving advice to people who were so much older than he. So Paul encouraged the young pastor with these words.

If you are young, you can do a good job. You may not have experience, but you have a brain. By being responsible, asking questions, and showing up on time and working a full day, you can do the work. Attend to the things you need to do every day, and your skill will grow. Use the things you already know and keep on learning, and soon people will forget how young you are.

After all, you won't always be this young, so make the most of the days you now have, knowing that God doesn't despise youth.

Lord, no matter what my age, I can always be a consistent
worker for You. Help me learn the things I need to do.

UNCHANGING

Jesus Christ is the same yesterday, today, and forever.

HEBREWS 13:8 NKJV

* * *

Change is constant in our world. In our jobs, clients change, technology changes, our bosses change. Sometimes we wonder when it will end and how we can keep up, over a whole career of revisions.

Some of us are "go with the flow" kinds who adjust easily to change; others like a lot of structure. But none of us can stay in the same place we are today. To do so would kill our careers—indeed, our whole lives.

As we seek to adjust to the world around us, it's nice to know that one thing *never* changes: Jesus. He does not give us one rule to live by today and eradicate it tomorrow. He never loves us one week and hates us the next. He says what He means and means what He says; all we have to do is read His Word to discover His truths.

So when work is up in the air, grab on to Jesus. He always has both feet on the ground. He's the unchanging Rock on which we can base our whole lives.

Lord, I need to plant both feet on You when the rest of my life is being rearranged. I'm glad You never change.

THE JOB HUNT

Ask, and it shall be given you; seek, and ye shall find;
knock, and it shall be opened unto you: for every one
that asketh receiveth; and he that seeketh findeth;
and to him that knocketh it shall be opened.

MATTHEW 7:7–8

•   •   •

Before you made the decision to look for a new job, you prayed about it. Certain this was what God wanted, you sent out your résumé, put out the word, and checked online to see what was available. If God is in this job hunt, how come you don't quickly have a new job? Did you misunderstand? Doesn't God want to give you good things?

God wants to give you the best. Just because He encourages you to do something doesn't mean it happens overnight. Sometimes it takes hard work to find a job; other times one just falls into your lap. The waiting may be part of what God is doing in your life, or the company you will work for may not be ready for you to start just now.

But whatever happens, God is in control. If you're doing your part, the job you finally land will be just the one He had in mind all along.

Lord, I want everything in my career
to glorify You, even a job search.

REST ASSURED

Six days thou shalt work, but on the seventh day thou shalt rest: in earing time and in harvest thou shalt rest.

EXODUS 34:21

❋ ❋ ❋

Your work is important, but fitting in a day of rest is even more significant. God vividly showed that to the Hebrews in this verse. After all, when you're a farmer with a crop to get in, you count every minute in the field. You need to get it safely stored before rain, bugs, or some other natural disaster can affect your crop.

God commanded people who had to live on their crops to take a day of rest, even in their busiest seasons. If they did not get the crop in, they would have a hard winter—perhaps even starve. This was a heavenly message they could hardly miss: they could depend on God to be sure they could bring in enough of their crop. Even if they lost some, He would provide for them.

Most of us don't face half a year's starvation if we rest on Sundays, but are we more likely than the Hebrew farmers to take a day off for rest and worship? Are we trusting in God less than they?

Lord, help me to spend Sunday with You in worship and rest.

CHOICES, CHOICES

So when Samuel saw Saul, the LORD said to him, "There he is, the man of whom I spoke to you. This one shall reign over My people."

1 SAMUEL 9:17 NKJV

* * * *

God chose Saul to rule His people. You'd think, with credentials like that, Saul would have to be a success. But though he started out well, Saul eventually became an example of what a king should *not* be.

Where did Saul go wrong? He became angry at the popular warrior, David, and at God. Saul constantly fueled his wrath and blamed God for his situation. Rather than asking God's prophet for advice, he turned to a medium. Soon the heavenly Father had no real place in Saul's life.

Each of us has success before us at some point. We start the new job, and everything looks promising. But in order to fulfill that promise, we need to continually make wise choices. What seems like a small choice one day may become a major stumbling block in a career if that decision was badly made. Pile up a series of poor choices, and a career suffers.

Don't make Saul's choices and lose the promise of your future to a moment of emotion.

Lord, help me make a success for You.
Don't let poor choices kill my promising career.

FOR THE RIGHT REASONS

*If you suffer, it should not be as a murderer or thief
or any other kind of criminal, or even as a meddler.*

1 PETER 4:15 NIV

* * *

Christians will suffer; the Bible makes no bones about that. But if a Christian's testimony is to be successful, he must suffer for doing the right thing, not because he has taken another's life. She must be accused wrongly, not because she has stolen. If that were not enough, Peter says a Christian should not even be rightly accused of meddling in another's business!

Can we be that pure on our own? It's not likely. Who among us has never felt like taking a coworker's life in our hands and "improving" on it?

As a Christian, at times you may suffer because of your faith. But let it be because you took a right but unpopular stand, not because you failed to do your work, harmed the company's image with dishonesty, or did wrong to your coworker. Instead, let God's Spirit control your life so completely that all people see is Jesus. Then the persecution they give you will really be aimed at Him.

What better company could you be in?

*Lord, when persecution comes, I want to face
it with You. Give me the strength of Your Spirit.*

THEFT IS THEFT

"If a man delivers to his neighbor money or articles
to keep, and it is stolen out of the man's house,
if the thief is found, he shall pay double."

EXODUS 22:7 NKJV

❋ ❋ ❋

When Alissa reported the theft of company property, she was amazed at the response she got. The security department called it "unauthorized removal" and never looked too hard for the culprits. But the loss of materials had cost the company a pretty penny. On top of that, she had to reorder everything since her department had planned to use the promotional materials to attract attention at a major convention. Not having them could have cost the company even more business.

We often don't take theft very seriously. We call it by other names to make it more appealing, and we excuse ourselves if we take home company property and never return it. But the Bible does not take stealing lightly. In the biblical era, when authorities caught a thief, he had to pay double for anything he had taken. Imagine paying twice the value for those pencils that ended up at home or the company T-shirt that wasn't given to you. It doesn't seem quite such a good deal now, does it?

Lord, keep me honest at work. I don't
want to take anything that isn't mine.

A WAY OUT

*The wife of a man from the company
of the prophets cried out to Elisha.*

2 KINGS 4:1 NIV

※ ※ ※

This woman was in a tight spot. Her husband died, and the man he owed money to planned to enslave her two sons. Without them, she'd have no financial support. So, in desperation, she cried out to God's prophet, Elisha.

God didn't tell the woman not to pay the debt. Her husband had gotten the money; it was only right that the creditor should be repaid. But He provided a way for her to pay. Elisha ordered the family to collect every pot they could from their neighbors. The woman poured oil in each, and the oil multiplied until it filled every vessel. Then the prophet told her to sell the oil and pay the debt.

When we don't live within our paychecks, we, too, can end up owing thousands. If we look for ways not to pay, God will not bless us. But He *will* help us pay if we ask Him—a second job or an affordable payment plan is a better solution than wrongdoing.

If you're in debt, trust God. He wants to provide for you, just as He did for that widow.

Lord, help me avoid debt and pay the ones I have.

LISTEN!

*The man of God sent word to the king of Israel: "Beware of
passing that place, because the Arameans are going down
there." So the king of Israel checked on the place indicated
by the man of God. Time and again Elisha warned the
king, so that he was on his guard in such places.*

2 KINGS 6:9-10 NIV

❀ ❀ ❀

Listening to God is of benefit, even if you are the person in charge.
We learn this lesson in a king who heard God by listening to His
prophet. During war with Aram, Elisha and King Joram worked as
a team. Because God told the prophet of the enemy's plans, Israel
constantly confounded the Arameans.

Are there battles you'd like to win on the job? Maybe you'd
like to feel secure about a new plan you're devising. Or you'd like
to know whom you can trust with some information. Ask God for
wisdom, and He'll provide it.

To hear, you have to be close to God. Anyone who does not
often pay attention to Him may expect a loud, booming reply. But
God rarely communicates that way. Only those listening to Him
day by day hear His still, small voice speaking to their hearts. Are
your ears completely open?

*Lord, help me listen to You every moment
so I can benefit from Your wisdom.*

UNDER PRESSURE

We were under great pressure, far beyond our
ability to endure.... But this happened that
we might not rely on ourselves but on God.

2 CORINTHIANS 1:8–9 NIV

* * *

Pressured days come to us all. Perhaps it's planned: a project you knew was coming but could not prepare for. Or maybe it's a sudden work overload. You wish there were more hours in the day, that you had more energy to complete your tasks—you aren't even sure how you'll find time to do laundry, eat meals, and take care of the rest of your everyday chores.

When pressure comes, rely on coworkers; it's good to share the load as much as possible. But even they may not take on enough to give you a forty-hour workweek. Then become deeply aware of your need for God's help. Without Him, you have no chance at completing the work. But God smooths your path and helps you make the most of your time.

Paul, who faced deadly perils much worse than our own, knew relying on God was his only chance. If he could trust God under such circumstances, then us trusting God should be a cinch.

Lord, I don't face Paul's dangers, but just like him, I can
rely on You. I need to trust that You will be with me in this.

CREATED FOR GOOD

For we are his workmanship, created in
Christ Jesus unto good works, which God hath
before ordained that we should walk in them.

EPHESIANS 2:10

* * *

When we create something, it feels good to know we've done a good job. As we put the final touches on a report, a letter, or whatever gadgets we make on the job, gladness fills us, not just that we've finished the job, but that we've done it well.

God enjoys creating things, too—like people. Imagine how He felt when He finished creating you. Did He smile, knowing He'd finished a masterpiece? Could He trust that here was a person who would do good works for Him out of deep love?

We may make a gadget and never see it again. A report or letter gets filed away. But that's not so with God; He sees us every day of our lives and watches us fondly as we do the good works He prepared for us to accomplish. When that work is finished, He calls us home because He made us and wants to share eternity with us.

Is the work you're doing today something that will make the Creator proud?

Lord, thank You for making me to do good things
that make You proud. Help me do those things today.

DO AS I DO

But I discipline my body and bring it into
subjection, lest, when I have preached to others,
I myself should become disqualified.

1 CORINTHIANS 9:27 NKJV

* * *

Paul recognized that preaching the Gospel meant more than telling people how to act. If he didn't live the words he preached, he would have no base to stand on. After all, if the apostle couldn't make Christianity work in his life, how could anyone else? If the man who had seen Jesus on the road to Damascus couldn't follow Him, how could the people of Corinth?

Paul's spiritual truth also applies to the workplace. What a leader says has some impact, but what he does will influence his staff even more. Managers who expect their staff to come in at an early hour had better be there at the crack of dawn, too. A CEO who expects her employees to take a pay cut had better not rake in a huge bonus at the end of the year.

The consistency Paul describes does not come easily. Living with congruity takes discipline, and discipline often goes against the grain with us. But before we break our own rules, we must look at the consequences. Is the risk of disqualification worth it?

Lord, I don't always like discipline,
but help me live consistently for You.

KEEP THEM IN YOUR PRAYERS

*I thank my God upon every remembrance of you, always in
every prayer of mine for you all making request with joy.*

PHILIPPIANS 1:3-4

* * *

Have you worked with some wonderful people? You spend so
much time on the job, chances are that you've made some work
friendships. Maybe you rarely see these folks outside of work, but
they still hold a treasured place in your heart.

If a coworker moves on to a new job, relocates to another state,
or retires, those fond memories remain with you. As you look back,
you may feel thankful, as Paul did when he thought of the Philippian
church. But do you also thank God and pray for that person?

As a caring Christian who believes God can work through
prayer, even when people are far distant, why not lift a special
workplace friend up to Him? Thank Him for that friendship. If you
still keep in touch, pray specifically for that friend's joys and needs.

You may not see your friend this side of heaven, but when
you meet again in eternity, the blessings of those prayers will
touch you both.

*Lord, I lift up my friend to You. Thank You for the love
You caused to flow between us, and bless my friend today.*

TAKE STOCK

Ye have sown much, and bring in little. . .and he that earneth
wages earneth wages to put it into a bag with holes.

HAGGAI 1:6

* * *

Sometimes, no matter how hard we work or how large our paycheck is, our ends don't seem to meet. No matter what we do, we have to pinch every penny.

Have we looked at our money issues as spiritual ones, or do we think money's too "practical" to relate to God? In this passage, God told the Jews their practical problems stemmed from a spiritual problem—they hadn't built His temple. They'd disobeyed Him and were paying a financial price.

Not every monetary problem stems from spiritual disobedience, but it's a good place to start. Take a spiritual inventory of your life. Did God warn you to control your spending, and you've kept on with it anyway? Or are you refusing to take part in the church's ministry? Ask yourself some deep questions and pray, being open to God's correction. Do what He directs you to do. Then live on whatever He provides, because when God provides, you'll make it through the end of every month.

Lord, show me any place I may not be in Your will.
Bring glory to Yourself even in my financial choices.

AN END TO WICKEDNESS

"He will cause deceit to prosper, and he will consider himself superior. When they feel secure, he will destroy many and take his stand against the Prince of princes. Yet he will be destroyed, but not by human power."

DANIEL 8:25 NIV

    ✳   ✳   ✳

Wicked power doesn't last. That was true in ancient Israel, and it's still true today.

Ancient Israel suffered under Antiochus IV, the Seleucid ruler described in this passage. He wanted to hellenize the Jews and began offending God's people by putting an altar dedicated to the Greek god Zeus in their temple. Many Jews did not respond as he expected, and his rule caused the Maccabean revolt, in which Israel rebelled against Greek rule.

Antiochus died a few years later, after Judas Maccabeus, leader of the revolt, had liberated Jerusalem. When Antiochus V, the next emperor, ended the persecution, all of Daniel's prophecy came true.

God won't let wicked governments last forever. It's as true today of corporate leaders as it was of ancient rulers. Those who do not follow moral practices are found out and eventually go under. So if your company is headed in a wrong direction and you want to keep your job, help set it on the right path.

*I don't want wickedness to prosper, Lord,
so help me to stand for what's right.*

WHAT'S YOUR REPUTATION?

A good name is rather to be chosen than great riches,
and loving favour rather than silver and gold.

PROVERBS 22:1

* * *

God says that a good reputation is valuable—more important than money. Today, it would seem He's got the minority opinion. But since God's truth never changes, we know that even if the rest of the world doesn't mind ruining their reputations, we need to value ours.

Reputations can come and go. You may get one when you take an unpopular stand, do something wrong, or make a mistake. Whether you've done something good or something wrong, unless it's something huge, that reputation usually passes with time.

But the reputation that does not stop is the one you build carefully—the one that shows what you wholeheartedly believe, the one you act on. Do right consistently, worship God with your whole life by following His will, and you will get a reputation worth keeping. Even if others don't like you for it, it will be better than "great riches" because it will earn eternal rewards.

I want a reputation for loving and serving You, Lord.
Guide me in making that happen.

IN A DIFFERENT LIGHT

But the men who had gone up with him said, "We can't attack those
people; they are stronger than we are." And they spread among
the Israelites a bad report about the land they had explored.

Numbers 13:31-32 NIV

* * *

Have you ever gone to a meeting and later heard two people's
responses to what went on? Amazing how different their takes
on it were, right?

People can be in the same place, see the same things, and
listen to the same words, and still not be able to agree on what
was said. Maybe that's what happened here. Faithful Caleb and
Joshua went up into Canaan and saw the lovely place God had
promised to lead them to. The doubting spies saw only huge,
dangerous people. The ten who brought back that bad report
ignored the riches of the land and only saw the inhabitants. Fear
overcame faith. So they reported out of their feelings, and God
calls their report evil.

When you hear differing reports, remember that people bring
their fear or faith into the workplace and see things in light of
them. You can't change their reports, but you can decide which
will influence yours—fear or faith.

Lord, help my report be a faithful one.

GOSSIP STOPS HERE

The words of a gossip are like choice morsels;
they go down to the inmost parts.

PROVERBS 18:8 NIV

❀ ❀ ❀

Let's face it—occasionally most of us like a good bit of gossip. We like to "hear the news" or "know what's going on." But what seems so tasty going down can give us an incredible case of indigestion.

Scripture says a lot about gossip—none of it good. God takes it seriously and never hands out exceptions for those things that we "just had to" pass on. Nor does He allow us to explain away our foolishness in bearing tales about other people, hurting their feelings, and ruining our own testimonies. So the next time someone offers you a "choice morsel" of gossip, let it end at you. Don't pass it on, talk about it to the person it concerned, or comment on it if someone else brings it up. Do all you can to defuse the situation by encouraging others to end it, too. Sometimes all it takes is one gently disapproving comment.

You'd appreciate it if others had a similar reaction when a story about you made the rounds. Let the meal end here, before it upsets more than one stomach.

Lord, give me strength to resist gossip in all its forms,
and help me make it stop with me.

SPIRIT OF PRAYER

Pray without ceasing.

1 THESSALONIANS 5:17

❀ ❀ ❀

How can I pray all the time? you may be wondering. *After all, I have to work, don't I?* Clearly you can't pray twenty-four hours a day; you do need some sleep! But that doesn't mean you can't engage in regular prayer for your company and coworkers. Remember them in your quiet time. Then, while you're doing one of those dull, mindless chores every job has, lift them up in prayer. Ask God to lead them in the right direction for decision-making or encourage them through trials.

The seventeenth-century monk Brother Lawrence called this attitude of prayer that follows you through the day "practicing the presence of God." While he worked in the monastery kitchen, with this method he brought himself and others before God.

You may not have much time to pray, but God responds even to lightning-quick intercessions. As you're walking to a coworker's office, waiting for a meeting to start, or on hold on the phone, remember your coworkers in prayer. Soon you'll find that even when you aren't praying, the spirit of prayer sticks with you—twenty-four hours a day!

Lord, keep me in prayer as often as I can be.
And don't let me forget my quiet time with You.

WITH JOY

Rejoice in the Lord always:
and again I say, Rejoice.

PHILIPPIANS 4:4

＊　＊　＊

Have you ever thought about the fact that knowing God is just plain fun? People who do not know Him often look upon God as being a big, mean judge, waiting to pounce down on them and cause them misery. They don't rejoice in God; in fact, they'd rather avoid Him because they know He has every right to judge them. It's not their idea of fun, and who could blame them?

One of the quiet testimonies you can offer to your coworkers is the joy you feel in God. You may not have to say a word, because they may not be able to miss your confidence in the face of trouble, the joy that bubbles up in you when you say His name, and the peace that covers you.

That doesn't mean you should never share your joy in words, as God leads you, but be aware that words alone are not enough to share God's love. Your spirit can shine even when words can't explain how you feel.

Lord, help my joy in You shine through. Thank You that You use my life even when I don't say a word. But help me speak joyfully of You, too.

RICH IN WISDOM

*Wisdom, like an inheritance, is a good thing and benefits those
who see the sun. Wisdom is a shelter as money is a shelter, but the
advantage of knowledge is this: wisdom preserves those who have it.*

ECCLESIASTES 7:11-12 NIV

* * *

Did you know that the money you make on the job is not what
keeps you alive? Sure, it pays the bills. But if you had to choose
between money and wisdom, wisdom is really the better choice.

Money comes and goes. And if you use your money wisely, it
will shelter you from hunger and homelessness. But if you don't live
wisely, you will end your life in misery. A lack of wisdom leads many
to make choices that lead them to illness, poverty, or emotional
trauma. In some cases, it can even lead to death.

But God's wisdom provides true life and protection, whether
you have plenty of cash or just a little. You might get some benefit
from money, but you will always benefit from wisdom, as it impacts
every portion of your life.

The only wisdom you need is what God has to offer. He'd love
to share it with you today. Are you ready to accept it?

*Lord, I need Your wisdom to make the
most of my life. Help me to walk in it today.*

HE WILL REPAY

God is just: He will pay back
trouble to those who trouble you.

2 THESSALONIANS 1:6 NIV

* * *

If you get the unfair part of a deal, if someone does you wrong, are you tempted to strike back? Does retribution look really good? It doesn't have to. God keeps in mind everything that's unfair, and in His own time, He works things out equitably.

So if you worked hard and didn't get a raise, don't take it out on the company. If a coworker spread gossip about you, don't do the same to him. Just leave it to God, and in a while, it will all make sense.

People who strike back at those who hurt them may seem to win in the short run, but eventually they, too, get a payback for their sin. So don't sin to get retribution; instead, rely on God, and if there is any retribution required, He will mete it out. Count on it; God's retribution will be perfect in a way yours never could be. When He hands out justice, it completely suits the situation, not too hard, not too soft. And the person who receives it gets the point of the lesson.

Lord, I don't want to strike back at those who do me wrong.
I know I can leave each situation in Your hands.

KNOW SCRIPTURE

*Now the Berean Jews were of more noble character than
those in Thessalonica, for they received the message
with great eagerness and examined the Scriptures
every day to see if what Paul said was true.*

ACTS 17:11 NIV

• • •

Derek had often heard Gil witness. The problem was that though
Gil was so emphatic about his beliefs, Derek knew they were not
quite scriptural. Sure, Gil quoted a lot from the Bible, but only
from the verses that supported his views. He ignored anything
that would prove him wrong.

When you're sharing the good news with coworkers, are you
sharing the whole news? Or like Gil, do you settle on a few verses
and ignore the rest of scripture? People need to hear a balanced
view of God that includes His justice and compassion. You can
best share that if you have a clear, broad understanding of the
Bible—one that comes from reading the whole book, Old and New
Testament. Read and study both, and then you can judge what you
hear to see if it's right or wrong.

Whether someone preaches to you or just shares his beliefs,
take it back to scripture. Then you'll know who is on target and
who's not.

*Lord, help me constantly learn from Your
Word so I can pass on a clear, full message.*

CELEBRATING LABOR

Then people go out to their work,
to their labor until evening.

PSALM 104:23 NIV

* * *

We put a lot of effort into our jobs, whether we work in a fast-food chain or an emergency room. And we have those jobs because someone needs what we do. We serve a purpose as we serve other people. Without our work, our country could not continue. Even if we don't get a lot of credit throughout the year, we are important to our bosses, our customers, and our world.

We may enjoy serving others and like to go to work each morning. But no matter how we feel about working, we all appreciate a day off, one that's designed to say to each of us, "Job well done!" Everyone should get some appreciation and praise at least one day a year.

So when Labor Day rolls around, even if your boss hasn't told you or your company hasn't said it, accept the compliment. You are important, and you do a worthwhile job. Well done!

Lord, thank You for this job You gave me.
I want to do well in it, and I appreciate the praise.

TRULY SUCCESSFUL

Those things, which ye have both learned, and received, and heard, and seen in me, do: and the God of peace shall be with you.

PHILIPPIANS 4:9

* * *

Cheri knew what was right, but she wasn't doing it. She tried to tell herself that God would understand. After all, He couldn't expect her to give up the fast track to success, could He? But as time went on and her doubts that this was okay increased, she felt more and more confused. What did God expect of her?

Obedience to God and His peace go hand in hand—you can't have one without the other. Paul told the Philippians that if they obeyed the truths God had shown them through the apostle, they would have peace because God would be with them.

Are you living in peace or worldly success that ignores the things you've learned about God? You can't have both. But you can live at peace with God and have a career that honors Him by following His commands. When you do that, no matter what job success you find, you'll be at peace.

Lord, I need to obey all I know of Your truth.
Keep me in Your way in every moment of my day.

THE VALUE OF A CUBICLE

*"There is more than enough room in my Father's home.
If this were not so, would I have told you that I
am going to prepare a place for you?"*

JOHN 14:2 NLT

* * *

Cubicles are a way of life in the working world, and though they make concentration a real challenge, maybe cubicles are one way God shows us how to get along well with others. If you work in cubicle space, you know that an inconsiderate conversation just outside your walls, as you're trying to concentrate, can become very irritating. If one offender has an office just around the corner, you may wish the speakers would do their talking in private.

Though offices are better for privacy than cubicles, cubicles can teach a lot of lessons about patience, consideration, and caring for others. God can use them to show us how to live well with others—even those who aren't wise or considerate.

Someday, in heaven, we'll have our own space. For now, let's learn to share our space with others.

Lord, let me learn a cubicle lesson here on earth.

PURE FOR CHRIST

But among you there must not be even a hint of sexual
immorality, or of any kind of impurity, or of greed,
because these are improper for God's holy people.

EPHESIANS 5:3 NIV

* * *

Though Sandra wasn't perfectly sure what her boss meant when he spoke those words, it sure sounded like an improper romantic suggestion. In only a moment, she'd gracefully but firmly refused. But the offense stuck with her. What had he been thinking? Sandra decided to say no more about it for the moment, but when her boss was fired some months later for other improprieties, she wasn't quite as shocked as her coworkers.

It's sad but true: some people will make such inappropriate comments in the workplace. When they open their mouths, it's time to speak up and to do so firmly. A Christian's only answer is no because Paul makes it clear that such wrongdoing should not be connected to God's holy people. Those whom Jesus has bought with His blood cannot take such actions lightly.

So if someone on the job says something immoral, deal with it quickly but as gently as possible. But be clear that you are saying no. To say anything else would foul the name of Jesus.

Keep me pure for You, Lord. I want to be holy for You.

GREEN WITH ENVY

Do not let your heart envy sinners,
*but always be zealous for the fear of the L*ORD.
PROVERBS 23:17 NIV

* * *

Does your heart turn green with envy when a coworker who doesn't know God buys a bigger house than yours or can afford to go to the best restaurant in town? It shouldn't, because your coworker may be settling for the riches of this world while bypassing more valuable eternal rewards.

Anyone who owns a huge house but has an empty heart is not completely blessed. Visit a well-to-do person who lives without Jesus and whose family problems have emptied his home of love, and that becomes apparent. But even the non-Christian with a happy family life only settles for an enjoyable eighty or so years, with no promise of eternal blessings.

The Christian who takes accountability to God seriously may not receive the earthly benefits of a large home or other extras. But giving to the church and Christian causes that made up that difference has been stored in heaven for all eternity.

Thank You, Lord, for eternal blessings that last more
than a lifetime. When greed tempts me, remind me that
I receive forever rewards when I do as You command.

"YOU FOOL!"

*You foolish Galatians! Who has bewitched you? Before your
very eyes Jesus Christ was clearly portrayed as crucified.*
GALATIANS 3:1 NIV

* * *

Have you ever felt like calling someone who works for you a fool?
Paul knew what that felt like—he became so irritated with the
Galatians that he all but called them that. But tactfully he said that
they must be bewitched, not their normal selves, to think that way.
He gave them an out, an excuse for their actions.

Paul knew what it was like to speak out honestly and even
offend people. He did it often enough in his ministry. So though
he speaks strongly, he also provides a tactful, hypothetical "excuse"
for the people who had missed the point of his ministry.

When you want to yell "fool" at someone, remember that after
you say that, you'll still need to work with your staff member. It's
probably better to hold your tongue on that name. Instead, explain
clearly what the problem is, and solve the issue that causes the
word to leap to your tongue. You'll be glad you spoke so wisely.

---

*Lord, help me hold my tongue on harsh words and
instead solve the real problem when a worker irritates me.*

BE HUMBLE

*When the turn came for Esther. . .to go to the king,
she asked for nothing other than what Hegai, the king's
eunuch who was in charge of the harem, suggested.
And Esther won the favor of everyone who saw her.*

ESTHER 2:15 NIV

* * *

Imagine a simple Jewish girl, a captive in Persia, being considered
for the position of queen. Esther knew nothing of palace life in a
strange land or how to please King Xerxes, who held her future
in his hands. Humbly, she recognized her need to rely on others
for wisdom. So Esther looked to Hegai for advice and not only
received the favor of all who saw her but won the heart of the king.

No matter your age or position, at times you need advice.
Like Esther, do you choose your counselors wisely? Then do you
follow their good advice, or does pride get in the way?

Humility often requires courage. We assume people will think
poorly of us if we admit we don't know all the facts or the best way
to proceed. But often just the opposite is true. Remember, too, even
when people undervalue humility, God never will. Perhaps that's
why He so often blesses the humble.

*Humility doesn't come easily to me, Lord.
Help me turn aside from pride and be meek instead.*

HIGHER ACCOUNTABILITY

"The God of Israel said, the Rock of Israel spoke to me:
'He who rules over men must be just, ruling in the fear of God.'"

2 SAMUEL 23:3 NKJV

● ● ●

Do you manage many people or just one? Then keep in mind that you are not simply accountable to your staff for how you lead. God is also concerned that you lead well.

This verse's description of leadership was among David's last words. The king wanted to tell his son Solomon the best way to rule. But his words apply not to kings alone. Anyone who has authority over others should keep them in mind.

Leaders who give God's opinion no credence easily get caught up in their own ideas and may become self-centered and opinionated. A leader who always has to be right, cannot forgive, or one with a low level of morality spells trouble for a company. One who does not care for the people he has authority over has trouble keeping a staff.

Ruling in the fear of God means wielding authority as one who is accountable to Him. Those who follow His rules, rule well.

Lord, help me rule well. I can only
do that as I keep Your rules in mind.

SAVED?

*"Run to and fro through the streets of Jerusalem; see now
and know; and seek in her open places if you can find a man,
if there is anyone who executes judgment, who seeks the truth,
and I will pardon her. Though they say, 'As the LORD
lives,' surely they swear falsely."*

JEREMIAH 5:1–2 NKJV

* * *

God couldn't find a truly just person in ancient Jerusalem, and
He isn't having an easier time today. In this sin-sick world, people
often say they believe in God, but you couldn't tell it by the way
they live. How can you know if a coworker who says he knows
Jesus really does?

None of us get to judge who goes to heaven. But the best
gauge on this side of eternity is a person's actions. If someone
who claims to share faith with you shows no evidence of a changed
existence, he may be missing the new life he claims.

Are you doubtful about another's faith? Share your own with
him. If he truly knows God, you may uncover hidden needs you can
help with. If he doesn't know the Savior, you may lead him to that
knowledge. Just a gentle witness can lead a wavering soul to truth.

*Lord, lead me not to judge, but to
bear Your witness everywhere I go.*

HONEST WEIGHTS AND WAYS

Dishonest scales are an abomination to the LORD,
but a just weight is His delight.

PROVERBS 11:1 NKJV

✦ ✦ ✦

Did you know that when you weigh out a product properly and charge your client the right price, God is pleased? *Could such a small thing really get the attention of God?* you may wonder. *It doesn't seem like much—could it really be that important?*

Yes, because God approves of honesty in all things. Over and over, scripture enjoins us to be honest people because living honestly reflects the kind of God we serve. Unlike some of the pagan gods, who were sometimes portrayed as sneaky, God does not play games with us. He tells us what He expects of us and stands by that expectation. As honest as He is with us is how He expects us to be with other people.

God hates any kind of dishonesty, so whether you are weighing out a product or charging a customer for a service your company provides, remember to be thoroughly honest. It's what you expect of Him, isn't it? And you don't want your actions to be abominable to God, do you?

Lord, make me honest in all my ways.

RUTHLESSNESS

A gracious woman retains honor,
but ruthless men retain riches.

PROVERBS 11:16 NKJV

❋ ❋ ❋

While the money is coming in, the ruthless think they've beaten the system. They've got it made, and no one can outdo them. But while they're selling their reputations cheap, the gracious woman, whom they have ignored or accused of naïveté, beats them on a front they've never even considered: the spiritual one.

Someday these ruthless men may find themselves envying the "naive" woman. She wasn't "important," until they needed her good opinion with others because those people have lost respect for them. But even more surely, there's a day when they will see her value, as, loaded with unforgiven sin, they face a holy God. Then they'll understand that they were the naive ones—thinking their sins would never find them out.

Over and over in scripture, God tells us sin will not escape Him (Exodus 32:33; Numbers 32:23; Psalm 69:5; Ezekiel 18:4). Do we really believe that? Or when we watch the ruthless ones, do we envy them? In a little while, face-to-face with Jesus, that envy will mean nothing as we glory in the right.

Lord, make me gracious, not ruthless. I want to please You.

A THORNY SITUATION

"But the sons of rebellion shall all be as thorns thrust away,
because they cannot be taken with hands. But the man who
touches them must be armed with iron and the shaft of a spear,
and they shall be utterly burned with fire in their place."

2 SAMUEL 23:6–7 NKJV

● ❄ ●

You can't deal nicely with a thorn—you either strip it off the plant or get rid of the plant entirely. Leaving thorn bushes to grow creates a sticky situation.

Rebellious people in the work environment are something like those bushes. Their anger flares up and attacks others and may keep them from performing their jobs well. Soon others, stuck with those thorns of anger, become resentful, and bitterness can quickly fill an entire department. Before it goes further, a wise leader removes rebellion by handling it with strong measures.

Leaders may not like this kind of action. It's easier to go with the flow than take a firm stand; but for the good of the entire company, it's best to confront the problem. A quickly solved situation has no time to grow into a sticky thorn bush.

Lord, when I deal with others, am I rebellious? Teach me
how to deal with those who have rebelled against You.

OUT OF PLACE

Like a gold ring in a pig's snout is a beautiful
woman who shows no discretion.

PROVERBS 11:22 NIV

❀ ❀ ❀

In these few words we get a clear message. This verse is a poetic way of saying someone can have physical loveliness that makes the world envious, but if she opens her mouth and spreads abroad the confidences people offer her, no one will think her beautiful. They'll recognize her weakness, and that one fact may well overwhelm everything else about her.

From Proverbs' pithy description, we also can imagine our innate reaction to this indiscreet human. We flinch away from her as we would a pig's gold snout ring. Beauty contrasting with ugliness can't make the entire person beautiful.

At work, people appreciate others who keep their private business private. Whether it's a business plan that isn't finished, information on a client, or a friend's personal life, when someone else would benefit by not having the word spread around, we need to keep the news private.

After all, we wouldn't want people to associate us with a pig, would we?

Keep my manners from being piggy, Lord,
by keeping me faithful to You. Remind me
that I have some things I'd like kept private, too.

KEEP YOUR COOL

*Human anger does not produce
the righteousness that God desires.*
JAMES 1:20 NIV

* * *

Anger burns in you for the wrong done to a coworker. How do you handle your emotions? Do you immediately attack the wrongdoers in an attempt to correct the wrong, or do you hold off, waiting for your emotions to cool?

When emotions burn hot, it's easy to think we need to correct that wrong immediately. We're in the right, after all, and such evil should not be allowed to exist. But if we open our mouths too quickly, we risk doing a worse wrong or being discounted because we cannot control our emotions. The good we seek to do is tossed aside by our bosses because we could not control how we felt.

Bringing about a righteous result doesn't take anger, but it may require a cool head and prayer. Emotions tend to beget emotions, so when you strike in anger, another person is likely to respond the same way. Instead of righteous solutions, you end up trapped in a circle of emotional turmoil.

No matter how good your intentions, don't use anger to try to please God. He says it'll never happen.

Lord, help me control my anger and seek Your solution instead.

LIKE THE THESSALONIANS

We remember before our God and Father your work
produced by faith, your labor prompted by love, and your
endurance inspired by hope in our Lord Jesus Christ.

1 THESSALONIANS 1:3 NIV

● ● ●

Face it, the Christian life is no piece of cake. Even Paul tells
the Thessalonians he remembers them for the energy they'd
expended on work, labor, and endurance. Certainly Christianity
in Thessalonica wasn't simple. The entire church faced persecution, just as Paul had when he first visited this bustling port.

But this church's efforts paid off. Paul used them as a model
for other congregations, to show how Christians should be, how
they should respond in troubles (vv. 7–10). Even today, we know
the Thessalonian church as one to be admired when it comes to
standing firm in trials.

Are you working, laboring, and enduring, while it seems to get
you nowhere? Don't give up. Keep on being a good testimony in
your workplace, and you may also become an example for others.
God may lift you up at the right time and use your example in a
powerful way.

Lord, I want my effort to be of benefit to You.
Keep me faithful all the way.

AFTER GOD'S OWN HEART

*"But now your kingdom will not endure; the L*ORD* has sought out*
a man after his own heart and appointed him ruler of his people,
*because you have not kept the L*ORD*'s command."*

1 SAMUEL 13:14 NIV

* * *

These words made Saul angry with God. Instead of waiting for the prophet Samuel, Saul had taken his place and offered a sacrifice. It was kind of like a low-level manager in your company speaking for the CEO without permission. Only no officer in your company speaks for God. Less-than-holy Saul had taken on a holy task. God was affronted that the proud king thought he could do this. So God decided He'd appoint a new leader who would love and respect Him.

Do we respect God in our work, or are we trying to do things our own way? If we have constant run-ins with authority, maybe we need to take a look at our attitudes. Have we gotten too much like Saul, who wanted it all his way?

Want your career to endure? Be like David, a person after God's own heart. It's the only way to be a successful leader—or a successful follower, if it comes to that.

Lord, keep me from being proud.
Instead I want to respect You in all I do.

PATIENCE, PLEASE!

Whoever is patient has great understanding,
but one who is quick-tempered displays folly.
PROVERBS 14:29 NIV

● ● ●

You're rushing to get through your day's work, and suddenly your computer program or some equipment goes kaput. *How will I ever get this done?* you ask yourself. In answer to that question, you have two choices: you can get upset, making solving the problem more difficult, or you can calm yourself, show patience, and think through a good solution.

Complaining to everyone around you may seem more fun than exhibiting patience, but unless you're explaining your problem to someone who can give you a solution, you're simply wasting time. Venting your anger in other ways isn't any better. You may feel relieved for a minute or so, but your problem waits back at your desk for you.

Patience and understanding work together to solve your problem. As you restrain your frustration, you can concentrate on understanding the problem and getting the help you need or deciding what's wrong so you can fix it.

Don't be a fool—let patience guide you instead.

Lord, help me keep my temper when frustration strikes.
Even then, I want to show faith.

DON'T GIVE UP

If any man see his brother sin a sin which is not
unto death, he shall ask, and he shall give
him life for them that sin not unto death.

1 JOHN 5:16

* * *

"I'm so disappointed in Joyce," Sarah admitted. "After all those years far from the Lord, she was walking with Him again, and now she's gone back to her old ways. I can't understand it."

It's hard when a Christian seems to forget the joys of knowing God and returns to sin. But we don't need to write that person off. Instead, God calls us to pray. What may seem to us to be the end of the story may be just another turn in the plot. God may have more work to do—and this could signify a time of humbling that will eventually reap spiritual benefits.

Know someone on the job who's turned in the wrong direction? Even if she won't listen, you can still bend God's ear on the subject. When He acts, you may see some real changes in your coworker's life.

Lord, work in the life of my coworker.
I want to see her living totally for You.

FAITHFUL TILL THE END

"Now give me this hill country that the LORD promised me that
day. You yourself heard then that the Anakites were there and
their cities were large and fortified, but, the LORD helping me,
I will drive them out just as he said."

JOSHUA 14:12 NIV

❋   ❋   ❋

Caleb was eighty-five years old when he requested this of Joshua. All those years he'd walked beside the faithless Israelites, and now he was coming into his own as one of only two Israelites who'd made it through all forty years of wandering. He and Joshua alone had come for a second time to the promised land.

How God blessed Caleb's steadfast faithfulness! When things were tough, Caleb believed. When they didn't go his way, he held on to God. Now the fruit of that faithfulness became reality, and Caleb received his inheritance. Though it was not easy, he was eager to continue in the Lord's service by conquering the land.

When we face challenges on the job, do we respond with Caleb's faith? Or do we let doubt overcome us if we don't see immediate results? However long we have to wait, God will not be faithless—we are the only ones who can be that.

Lord, keep me faithful to You,
no matter how long I have to wait.

ONE OR THE OTHER

Can the fig tree, my brethren, bear olive berries? either a vine,
figs? so can no fountain both yield salt water and fresh.

JAMES 3:12

＊ ＊ ＊

When you're on the job, do you allow yourself to become involved in practices that displease God and still expect to please Him on Sunday? If so, you probably feel frustrated with your Christian walk. You may even be tempted to say that Christianity "doesn't work."

There's a reason why that kind of "faith" doesn't work. God says that if you're a fig tree, you bear figs, not olives. Either you're going to do good to honor Him or you'll do the acts of wickedness that show where your true allegiance is. You can't do some of both and be a true Christian testimony.

Christians, James says here, have to be consistent. They'll either be sweet, potable water or salt water that kills all growth. If you're trying to do some of both, is it time to find a new job—or even a new line of work—where you don't have to compromise your Christian faith? Or is it time to simply begin living the way you know you should?

Lord, I don't want to try to be two things at once.
Help me live for You at work and church.

THE DIFFICULT RESPONSE

*But I say unto you, Love your enemies, bless them that
curse you, do good to them that hate you, and pray for
them which despitefully use you, and persecute you.*

MATTHEW 5:44

* * *

You could respond to a nasty coworker in a lot of ways. You might
become so irritated that you quit your job; or you could treat that
person like dirt to get even; or you could love him as Jesus does
and pray daily for him.

The first response might be giving up too easily; the second
is clearly wrong. But following this biblical advice, while more
difficult, could make some big changes in your attitude—and
your coworker's. Though you may not end up being best friends,
as you pray for and love that person, God can begin to work in
your relationship to disarm the nastiness. Though it may seem
impossible, God can make you at least tolerate each other. Let
Him control your feelings and reactions, and you'll be amazed at
the work He can do. Prayer really works!

*Lord, help me love my enemy today. Give me the patience and
strength, because I know I can't do it under my own power.*

GOD OR MAN?

"Do not be afraid of those who kill the body
but cannot kill the soul. Rather, be afraid of the
One who can destroy both soul and body in hell."

MATTHEW 10:28 NIV

* * *

Your boss tells you to lie. You know it's wrong, but will he fire you for disobedience? He'd have every right to.

At this point, you have a choice. You can obey your boss, who can control your working life but not your eternal destiny or the rewards that go with it, or you can obey God. It's a tough choice if you have a family to feed, but it may not be as impossible as you think. Because when God calls you to obey Him, He also provides for you. That provision may be a new job, even if it follows a time of unemployment. Or the situation may come to a head, and your boss may change his mind or be reprimanded by someone higher up.

But whatever the choice you need to make, you can be sure you've made the right one if you follow Jesus. He holds eternity, not just your nine-to-five life, in His hands.

When I'm challenged to tell the truth, Lord,
keep me faithful to You. I trust You with my whole life.

SERVE TO LEAD

"But it is not to be this way with you; on the contrary, the one who is the greatest among you must become like the youngest [and least privileged], and the [one who is the] leader, like the servant."

LUKE 22:26 AMP

❀ ❀ ❀

Most people like to lord it over people in their power. They often think of them as being "below" them. But Jesus made it perfectly clear to those who would lead the fledgling church that this was not the way they were to deal with others. The name of Christian leaders is not "boss," but "servant." Those who want to be greatest must put others ahead of themselves.

If you've worked for people with this philosophy, you've probably been a happy employee. Having someone who makes your job easier by providing you with the tools, information, and encouragement to do your job well is a wonderful thing. Count your blessings if you work for such a person.

If you don't work for such a person, make certain you become the first example of servant leadership in your place. The same idea that worked in the church will work in the "real world," too.

Lord, help me to serve those I work with and work for.

PRESS ON!

Not that I have already obtained all this, or have
already arrived at my goal, but I press on to take
hold of that for which Christ Jesus took hold of me.

PHILIPPIANS 3:12 NIV

* * *

Some days it's tough to press on. Work isn't exciting. Life is hard or dull. We wonder why we do what we do and where it will lead us. If the weather's beautiful or we have something better to do at home, we may wonder what we're doing in the office or at the factory.

Why don't we just skip out? Maybe it's because even when we'd like to be sunning ourselves or working on a project at home, we have a commitment that won't let us escape from doing the right thing. Like Paul, we aren't perfect, but we're on the path to holiness, and that includes doing right by our employers.

Holiness isn't an overnight thing—Paul didn't find it so, and neither do we. It comes to us in bits and pieces as we follow Jesus day by day. The more we seek to please Him, the more our lives slowly transform.

Jesus has grabbed ahold of you. Are you grabbing ahold of Him, too?

Lord, I'm holding on tight. I need to
be more and more like You—perfect.

TRUSTED

"You are to bring into the ark two of all living creatures,
male and female, to keep them alive with you."

GENESIS 6:19 NIV

* * *

By the time Noah had all the animals in the ark, he was probably realizing what a huge job God had given him. But God had also given him a lot of trust. Without his care, some kinds of animals would no longer exist—he could have wiped out a species by simple carelessness.

When your job seems overwhelming, do you appreciate the trust that's placed in you? Whether you hold people's lives in your hands or do a more mundane job, your work is important to someone. How you carry it out is at least important to your boss—and God, who may not care if you flip burgers or do brain surgery but who wants you to do your work to the best of your ability.

Appreciate the trust that goes with your job, whatever level you're on, and do your work to God's glory as well as for a paycheck.

Let me work to Your glory, not just for my own needs, Lord.

MAKE THE BEST OF IT

This pleased Potiphar, so he soon made Joseph his
personal attendant. He put him in charge of his
entire household and everything he owned.

GENESIS 39:4 NLT

❋ ❋ ❋

Thrown into a pit by his brothers, sold into slavery to Ishmaelite traders—a state of affairs that barely saved him from death at his siblings' hands—Joseph had some tough breaks. When he reached Egypt and was sold to one of Pharaoh's officers, things looked pretty bleak for the young Hebrew.

But Joseph didn't spend a lot of time whining and complaining. He didn't go on strike because he had become a slave but deserved better. Instead he drew close to God, and God blessed him (v. 2). His work went amazingly well, to the point where Potiphar noticed. The more God blessed the slave, the more authority he received in Potiphar's household, until Joseph was running everything.

If you face difficulties at work, do you complain or despair? Or do you draw close to God and do your best? The first response won't get you far, but the second could benefit both you and your workplace. Be a Joseph on your job.

Lord, when I face work challenges and doubts,
help me, like Joseph, to remain faithful to You.

GODLY RISKS

*"I will go with you," said Deborah. "But because of the
course you are taking, the honor will not be yours."*

JUDGES 4:9 NIV

* * *

God gave Barak a message through Deborah. He was to fight his
enemy, Sisera, and God would give the Canaanite commander
into Barak's hands. But nervous Barak wanted security—certainty
that Deborah was right and God would do what she said. He'd
only obey if she came with him. God granted Barak's desire, but
because the Israelite commander lacked trust, Deborah told him
a woman would kill Sisera and get the credit for it.

In the workplace we, too, sometimes want both the security
and the glory when our company lands a big contract. We don't
want to risk a lot on the sale, but we want the raise or bonus after
the job comes through. Just like Barak, we can't have our cake
and eat it, too.

We shouldn't take every risk that's out there—it would be
foolish to do so. But when we have looked at every angle and the
risk seems worth it, when we've prayed about our decision-making
and feel that doing this would please God, it's not time to hold
back. It would be foolish not to listen.

*Lead me, Lord, when I face risks.
I need Your guidance every day.*

GOD IS IN CONTROL

The king's heart is in the hand of the LORD, like the
rivers of water; He turns it wherever He wishes.

PROVERBS 21:1 NKJV

* * *

Do you worry about decisions your boss, the government, or industry giants make that influence your working life?

Take comfort, then, in this verse. No matter what powerful person makes choices that influence your life and work, no decision, even from the rankest unbeliever, is beyond God's planning and mercy. Though you may disagree with the choices of the powerful or consider their judgments unwise, though their decisions may have made your life more difficult, nothing surprises God or disturbs His plan for your life. The All-Powerful One really has all authority, ultimately even over those who do not believe in Him.

So if you start to worry, don't get caught up in a spiral of emotional defeat. Instead, pray for those corporate executives, government decision-makers, and titans of industry. God may work through your prayers to turn their hearts and minds, like a river, to a better resolution.

I put my life in Your hands, Lord, and ask that You give wisdom
to the decision-makers in my company and industry.
I ask that You might guide their way today.

SAINTED

Yea, he loved the people; all his saints are in thy hand: and they sat down at thy feet; every one shall receive of thy words.

DEUTERONOMY 33:3

* * *

Did you know that if you have faith in Jesus, God calls you a saint? No one has to find miracles you've done or show just how holy you are in order for you to receive that name. A biblical saint is a "holy one," someone called to show the difference God makes in human lives by being set apart for Him.

Some liturgical churches have named a select few saints, and many of them have exciting Christian testimonies to be shared with the world. The biblical saints Peter, Paul, John, and so on started the newborn church on its path. In the Middle Ages, Saint Patrick and Saint Columba helped spread the Gospel to new lands. We can rightly admire their faith and work.

But let's not allow our less-exciting testimonies to make us feel so inferior that we never reach a hurting modern workplace, where those without hope surround us. The ancient truth bearers are not the only ones God wants to use. Are you showing the world His difference through your life?

Lord, I'm honored to be one of Your saints. Let me bear Your light to those I work with today.

COVET NOT

Let your conversation be without covetousness;
and be content with such things as ye have: for he
hath said, I will never leave thee, nor forsake thee.

HEBREWS 13:5

* * *

Who among us would not be glad to receive some more money? We can always find a "good" use for it, whether it's fixing up the house or going on vacation. What's wrong with that?

The problem isn't in the money; it's in the attitude people have about it. Some can live contentedly on what they make, though they'd never turn down a raise or windfall. Others are like the overweight person who doesn't eat to live but lives to eat. The person with a money problem has made money the focus of life and will no longer be content with "enough." Make more, and still it's not enough.

Instead of loving money, the Christian appropriately loves the one who provides it. Money may come and go, but Jesus doesn't. When the checking account is empty, He never is. When the assets are frozen, He's still offering a warm heart. So don't love money, but the one who really controls it. His name isn't your bank president's or Uncle Sam—it's Jesus.

Lord, I know You provide all I have.
Thanks for what You've given me.

GOD GOALS

I press toward the mark for the prize of
the high calling of God in Christ Jesus.
PHILIPPIANS 3:14

* * *

Though you may never list them on a piece of paper, you have career goals. You may want to stay in your field for the rest of your career and rise up the ladder in your company. Or, dissatisfied with your work, you may be looking for a new calling.

But while you focus on your career goal, do you miss out on an even better goal that will end in more than a good 401(k) plan or accolades? Are you keeping your eye on service to God?

You can and should serve God on the job. But are you also giving Him the rest of your day? God provides you with spiritual gifts He does not intend to be left on a shelf, stuck behind a dusty Bible. That would be like ignoring your boss from nine to five. Instead, your use of your "spare time" should earn a prize with God.

Are you pressing on to God's high calling or being a spiritual couch potato?

Keep my eye on the goal of serving You with
my whole day, Lord. I want to honor You.

OBEY WITH EYES OPEN

Servants, be obedient to them that are your masters
according to the flesh, with fear and trembling,
in singleness of your heart, as unto Christ.

EPHESIANS 6:5

* * *

Obeying your boss can be a pleasure or a curse, depending on what kind of boss you have. When you feel part of a team and know that your obedience will benefit your entire company, it's easy to obey. If your boss offers excellent leadership, you want to do the right thing.

But what about the days when you wonder if obeying will be a good thing? Do you hold your peace and obey blindly, or do you open your mouth and perhaps put your foot in it?

The best place to start is by lifting up your situation to God. Don't begin a prayer marathon, but briefly ask for guidance. If you can wait a bit, it might be best to hold off an hour or two because sometimes such problems solve themselves. Then if you can, chat with your boss about your doubts.

But ultimately, God holds you responsible for obedience. So if your boss holds firm and what you're doing doesn't go against God's Word, follow your boss's direction. Trust that God is in control of everything—even your boss's choices.

Lord, help me obey—but not blindly.

JUST BELOW THE SURFACE

*Exhort bondservants to be obedient to their own masters,
to be well pleasing in all things, not answering back.*

TITUS 2:9 NKJV

❋ ❋ ❋

You know what it's like. While you're trying so hard to say the right things, awful words trip off your tongue. It's so strange, you feel like turning around and asking, "Where did that come from?" You'd had thoughts on the subject but never intended to share them publicly. Now here your doubts are, out there for your boss and everyone else to see.

Eventually the things on our hearts and minds come out somehow. The ideas, hurts, and fears that bubble below our conscious level churn up unexpectedly, perhaps at the most troublesome moments. It can be embarrassing when they show up in our speech.

Avoid such incidents by clearing up each problem while it's small. Deal with minor concerns, and they'll never become major. Instead of waiting for bitterness or anger to trip off your tongue, confront your boss before final decisions are made, when you can have input and changes can be made. This may keep you from making a huge mistake that will affect your career. Better than that, you'll be pleasing God, too!

*Lord, keep my tongue in check and
let every word I speak please You.*

CHOOSE YOUR BATTLES

And David enquired of God, saying, Shall I go up against the Philistines? and wilt thou deliver them into mine hand? And the LORD said unto him, Go up; for I will deliver them into thine hand.

1 CHRONICLES 14:10

* * *

While David fought and fled from King Saul, he learned a good lesson: everyone has to choose which battles to fight and which to avoid. The anointed but not crowned king also knew where to go for the wisdom to make such decisions: God alone was his adviser.

We may not fight against warriors, but we also need to choose our battles. On the job, we face issues that are not important enough to be fought over. Disputing about a vacation day that you and a coworker both want to take has no long-term value. Trying to replace the boss's son on a job will be a losing battle.

As we face battles large and small, we, too, need to look to David's source for guidance. Instead of relying on our own wits and wisdom, as we turn to God, we can know where our efforts will be most effective. When God sends us on a mission and we follow His direction, our battles will be won.

*Lord, help me choose which battles
to engage in and which to avoid.*

PUT TO GOOD USE

*Stay away from all believers who live idle lives
and don't follow the tradition they received from us.*
2 THESSALONIANS 3:6 NLT

※ ※ ※

Is there such a thing as a good Christian lazybones? Not according to Paul. He made it perfectly clear that he didn't appreciate some Christians sitting around and awaiting the second coming in frivolous living, sticking their noses in other people's business and expecting others to support them (vv. 11–12).

It's one thing to be temporarily unemployed and another not to work and to expect never to work. Not using your hands in a worthwhile fashion does not make you a better person. Paul says just the opposite when he tells Christians not to become friendly with those who have this attitude.

God anoints hard work done for Him. Think of the blessed people of the Bible. Can you think of one who did not work? Noah kept a whole zoo for months and months; Deborah judged her people; David ruled a nation; Paul and the other apostles spread the Gospel to much of the known world. They didn't sit on their hands, waiting for whatever God planned.

Putting our lives in God's hands doesn't mean we do nothing. Instead we do all He puts in our hands.

Lord, give me something to do for You today.

ENSLAVED TO CHRIST

For he who is called in the Lord while *a slave is the Lord's freedman. Likewise he who is called* while *free is Christ's slave.*

1 CORINTHIANS 7:22 NKJV

❋ ❋ ❋

In the Roman Empire, slaves held down many jobs, including the ones we'd consider professional. Scribes, farmworkers, and teachers could all be slaves. Though slavery wasn't as common in Paul's homeland, the Corinthians would have had a sharp mental image of what he was talking about.

Paul told them that no matter whether they were slaves or free, they'd had to serve someone. Before they'd known Jesus, they served Satan, who controlled them no less than a wicked master who forced them to do his will. Now, though they served a kinder master in Jesus, they were just as obligated as they'd been before.

Today, we may punch information into computers, guide a train into a station, or fly above the earth on our jobs, but we're still obligated to obey someone. Are you obeying Jesus or only calling Him Lord and giving your life to the evil one?

Lord, I want to be Your slave, no one else's.
Help me serve You on the job and in the rest of my world.

LETDOWN

I went out full, and the LORD hath
brought me home again empty.

RUTH 1:21

* * *

Ramon started a new job, and everything looked so wonderful. The company's promises for promotion looked good, and he was heading in the career direction he'd always wanted to go. He couldn't wait to jump into work.

It didn't take Ramon long to see that what he thought he was getting into and what he really had to deal with were two different things. It wasn't that the company had lied to him, but his new boss just didn't seem to realize exactly how things were in the marketplace. After only a few weeks on the job, Ramon could see he'd better start looking again.

Sometimes a new job doesn't work out. Much as job hunting may be tough, it may be best to leave that place and look for a new one or to look around while you hold on to that less-than-wonderful position.

When something like this happens, it's easy to ask, "Where was God in all this?" Don't assume God has abandoned you. He may be taking you on a longer path, but He hasn't forgotten your needs. In the end, empty or full, He'll bring you home.

Lord, when I wonder where You are,
remind me that You're right beside me.

STILL ON THE CLOCK

Six days shalt thou labour, and do all thy work.

EXODUS 20:9

* * *

Those "down" times of slow work, when you have little or nothing to do, prove why busyness, as irritating as it can be, is not the worst state of affairs to be in.

What do you do during your downtimes? Clear out unnecessary e-mails? Catch up on filing? Do all the boring chores you've put off for a while? Remember, your company pays you—even when business is slow. So as long as you have something to do, keep working. Be as faithful as possible in putting in your required hours.

When you completely run out of anything to do, can you help another department that's bogged down? If your offer is turned down, do something quiet so you don't disturb those who *are* working.

Remember, God has only given you so many days to work; and while you're working, He expects you to do your best. How else could you effectively honor Him?

Lord, make me a dedicated worker, even in downtimes. Don't let me take advantage of what should be my boss's claim on my time.

A SOFT ANSWER

*And when Peter came up to Jerusalem, those
of the circumcision contended with him, saying,
"You went in to uncircumcised men and ate with them!"*

ACTS 11:2-3 NKJV

* * *

No sooner did Peter get back from a business trip than his fellow apostles were complaining about the job he'd done. To a Jew, eating with pagans was wrong, and they couldn't imagine why Peter had done this. What was he thinking? Was Peter going to set a bad precedent here? What could come of it? But instead of tactfully asking, they jumped down his throat.

You may know what it's like to be on the receiving end of similar criticism. It's a human failing to attack first and ask questions later. When it happens, do you follow Peter's example in the next verses and explain? Do you publicly ignore the talebearers who told your management what you did and speak graciously to everyone involved? Do you deal privately with anyone who did wrong? By reacting this way and not in anger, the apostle turned the situation around and gained the agreement he was seeking. A soft answer is the best answer when attacks come your way.

Lord, help me speak softly but clearly when I'm attacked.

LET GOD EXALT

Though thou exalt thyself as the eagle,
and though thou set thy nest among the stars,
thence will I bring thee down, saith the LORD.

OBADIAH 1:4

* * *

The accounting firm of Arthur Andersen was one of the most successful in the business when some sheets of shredded paper changed the whole company's future. Not only that, the wrongdoing of one employee became the basis of the damaging lawsuit that named the entire company liable and forced it to reorganize on a smaller scale. One choice to shred papers that would have shown Enron's real financial status and uncovered the criminal acts within the company cost thousands of people their jobs in both companies.

The next time you think your actions won't reflect on the company as a whole, think again. You probably aren't doing something illegal, but are you representing your company as being proud, uncaring, or rude? Don't let current success make you think nothing can change. Though you're flying like an eagle today, God can bring you down if you slide into evil.

Let God's Spirit be the wind that lifts your career on high, and He will never bring you down. Be exalted in Him, not in a company's profit sheet or positive reputation.

Lord, lift my career up so it will glorify You.

MOTIVATION, GOD'S WAY

*Whoever pursues righteousness and unfailing
love will find life, righteousness, and honor.*
PROVERBS 21:21 NLT

❋ ❋ ❋

While managers often spend a lot of time trying to find ways to
motivate their staff to do better work, God is *the* expert at motivating people. He sets the agenda, then offers generous rewards. His
plan is evident in this verse. "Follow My way, and I will bless you
with life, righteousness, and honor," He says.

Notice the large size of the benefits. God doesn't offer a
onetime reward, a pat on the head, or a big promise that's never
fulfilled. Those who follow Him earn lifetime blessings that affect
them forever. He also doesn't give people things they don't want
or need—another vacation day when they'd prefer the cash or
cash when they'd rather take a vacation. The benefit is uniquely
suited to the need.

If you're a manager trying to motivate your staff, consider
what they really want or need. You may not be able to fulfill every
wish, but chances are there is something they'd like, whether it's
a more positive work environment or financial compensation.

*Lord, thank You for giving me the best motivation.
Whether I'm working with staff or encouraging
another worker, help me give just what's needed.*

CYNICAL HEARTS

*He said to them, "Listen to this dream I had: We were
binding sheaves of grain out in the field when suddenly
my sheaf rose and stood upright, while your sheaves
gathered around mine and bowed down to it."*

GENESIS 37:6–7 NIV

❋ ❋ ❋

Seventeen-year-old Joseph had an amazing dream he couldn't
wait to share with his brothers—he was going to be great! When
this young man told his siblings what he'd dreamed, he got a great
shock. His brothers didn't like the idea that they would serve him.

Like Joseph's experience, work has a way of making us realists.
It wakes us up to the way other people think and feel. We learn
to take account of coworkers' strengths and weaknesses, as well
as our own.

Becoming realistic in the work world is fine, as long as we
don't become cynics. Joseph easily could have become one when
his dream led his brothers to sell him into slavery. He worked
many difficult years before that dream came true. Though he lost
his naïveté, Joseph remained faithful to the God who gave him the
dream. Joseph developed realism aplenty, but never a hard heart.

Can we say the same of ourselves?

*Lord, make me a realist, not a cynic.
I want my heart to be all Yours.*

DON'T PUT A LID ON IT!

*"Let more work be laid on the men, that they may
labor in it, and let them not regard false words."*

EXODUS 5:9 NKJV

* * *

This was Pharaoh's method of keeping his Hebrew slaves out of
trouble: pour so much work on them that they'd be exhausted and
unable to listen to Moses. Though it may have controlled his slaves
for a short time, the ruler could almost have counted on rebellion
breaking through. It was as if he'd put a lid on an overfilled, boiling
pot but not taken the fire from under it.

Quelling trouble or solving problems with oppression doesn't
work for long because it doesn't bring about change. Emotions rise
as people feel they've been wronged, and the situation escalates.
It was true for Pharaoh, and it's true for us today. Putting a lid on
the problem never solves it.

Have a work-related problem you want to end? Don't use
Pharaoh as your management expert and put a lid on it. Solve the
underlying problem instead.

---

*Lord, help me find a solution for my problem,
instead of trying to control others.*

HELP!

I say then: Walk in the Spirit, and you
shall not fulfill the lust of the flesh.

GALATIANS 5:16 NKJV

* * *

"I just can't do this on my own. It's overwhelming!" Have you ever thought or spoken those words on the job? If so, you were crying out for help.

Work isn't the only place we face an overwhelming need for help. Sometimes we require it in our spiritual lives, too. We've tried to be good and do the right thing. We want to serve Jesus alone, but temptation keeps getting in our way. We can't get the best of it, though we pray, study scripture, fellowship with other believers, and ask their advice. Nothing seems to work.

Overcoming sin isn't our job. If it were, it would be a hopeless one. It's the Spirit who works on sin in our lives. Where all our efforts fail, His gentle touch works a miracle of grace.

As we throw ourselves on God's mercy, admitting our own need and helplessness, the Spirit can enter our spirits and work that grace. When we completely offer up our sin-battered lives to Him, He changes them entirely.

Lord, I need help! Only You can
free me from this sin. Take my life now.

NUMBERING THE HOURS

So teach us to number our days,
that we may apply our hearts unto wisdom.

PSALM 90:12

● ● ●

Numbering your days is fine, but do you often feel as if you have to number your hours? There's so much to get done in a weekend. Life tends to get crammed full. Every moment has something going on.

Maybe numbering our hours isn't such a bad idea. After all, hours make up the days, and God only gives us so many days to our lives. We need to consider the fact that we'll only spend so many of them on earth. So each hour should count for something.

That doesn't mean we should never rest. Everyone needs downtime. But it needs to be productive downtime that recharges our batteries, not simply another event to add to our to-do list.

Perhaps that means we put off the major league event and go to the backyard instead to throw a ball with our kids, or maybe it means taking a nap so we refresh our bodies. But whatever we do this weekend, may every hour be of benefit to someone else or ourselves. It's only wise to plan what we do.

Lord, I want to use my time on earth wisely.
Show me every hour just what to do.

WHAT A CRUMMY DAY!

This is the day which the Lord hath made;
we will rejoice and be glad in it.

PSALM 118:24

⁂

Having a bad day? This morning you woke up tired and grumpy, and things haven't gone right from that moment. You took the dog out and he wouldn't come back in, so you spent a lot of time coaxing him into the house. Either you didn't have time for breakfast, or it burned. Traffic on the way to work was horrific. Now you've opened up your computer, and it's not working.

We all have days that go awry, ones where we'd like to be able to go back to bed, pull the covers over our heads, and sleep away twenty-four hours. If only we didn't have to work on them!

It's hard to recognize on tough days that this, too, is a day God made and one He made to benefit us. But unless the day is already gone, it's not beyond repair. Turn around your less-than-impressive days by giving them back to God. He knows what you're going through and wants to help, but He won't barge in. Ask Him to take over those awful twenty-four hours, and you will be able to rejoice in them.

Lord, take this day and make of it what You will.

IN GOD WE TRUST

*His ways are always prosperous. . . He says to himself, "Nothing
will ever shake me." He swears, "No one will ever do me harm."*

PSALM 10:5-6 NIV

❀   ❀   ❀

Did you know that most people think a 20 percent raise is all it
would take to make them happier? Just that much money and
they could be really at peace, cover all their bills, and maybe even
give a little more.

But if you've been working for a number of years, you should
know the falseness of that idea. You've received 20 percent more
money, and it hasn't solved all your financial problems. It hasn't
been a quick solution to every trial.

The prosperous fellow described in these verses is evil; he
thinks God has forgotten people (v. 11). So he places his trust in
his house and lands, his bank account, and the other things he
owns. When he thinks worldly goods have made him happy, he's
deluding himself. He makes more and more, owns more and more,
yet never finds peace.

If you get a raise, rejoice. Be glad God has provided, but don't
trust in the things He's given instead of the one who's given them.

*Lord, I want to trust in You, not money or things.
Keep me faithful always.*

THE RULE ABOUT RULES

For verily I say unto you, Till heaven and earth pass, one jot or one tittle shall in no wise pass from the law, till all be fulfilled.

MATTHEW 5:18

＊ ＊ ＊

The Pharisees were zealous about rules—they could identify every single Old Testament rule (and more that weren't there) and demanded that people follow each. In the process of seeking to know God on their own terms, they lost out on the real meaning of His forgiveness.

When Jesus came along, He made the Pharisees nuts. Here He claimed to be God, yet He didn't know how to keep score "properly." The legalism that meant so much to the Pharisees was foreign to His nature. When Jesus said He fulfilled the Law, the Pharisees must have been livid.

Rules are needed in any workplace. They're guidelines that keep everyone working together. But just as the Old Testament Law was designed to show God's holiness and love, not create a "who can top this?" game, rules aren't meant to be the be-all and end-all of work.

Follow the rules, but don't make a god of them. God isn't just a rule maker. He's using His law to show you how much He cares.

Today, Lord, show me how to use rules wisely.

LOST AND FOUND

*And when she hath found it, she calleth her friends
and her neighbours together, saying, Rejoice with me;
for I have found the piece which I had lost.*

LUKE 15:9

❁ ❁ ❁

If you've lost an important piece of paperwork, then found it in an odd place, you know the joy this woman felt. While you rushed around looking for it, tension mounted. But when you found it, your whole body relaxed. Joy flooded your emotions.

Just like your paperwork or the coin the woman in the story found, you are important to your heavenly Father. While you're lost spiritually, He feels concern. He seeks you out to bring you home to heaven. When you turn to Him and enter His kingdom, He sets His angels to rejoicing. The tension concerning your salvation is finished, and your forever home is chosen.

We understand the importance of paperwork that's key to a project or a coin that provides for earthly needs. But do we comprehend the importance of a soul to Jesus? It's so easy to assume the lost person will never accept the Lord and will bypass Him. The search for that soul seems harder than finding a lost coin or paper.

But what fun to rejoice when that person is saved!

Lord, I'd rather rejoice. Help my testimony lead others to You.

ADMIT IT!

"Pick me up and throw me into the sea," he replied,
"and it will become calm. I know that it is my fault
that this great storm has come upon you."

JONAH 1:12 NIV

✳ ✳ ✳

Jonah knew he'd made a mistake before he even reached land. Out in the middle of the sea, a storm hit. When the other passengers on the ship cast lots and discovered he was the cause of their trouble, the prophet immediately admitted to it. Jonah was willing to have them toss him into the sea just to save the vessel.

When we make mistakes, are we willing to do whatever it takes to make them right? Jonah might not have wanted to go to Nineveh, but neither did he want his disobedience to cost the lives of his fellow travelers. He took responsibility for the wrong and found a way to fix it, even at the cost of his own life.

Everyone makes mistakes on the job, but not many are brave enough to admit them. That doesn't mean the boss can't figure it out, just that it takes a little more time or effort. Admit to your mistakes, and maybe, like Jonah, you'll find that your coworkers aren't in a rush to slip you over the side.

Lord, help me be humble enough to admit my mistakes.

TAME YOUR INNER REBEL

Woe to [Jerusalem], rebellious and defiled!
She obeys no one, she accepts no correction. She does
not trust in the LORD, she does not draw near to her God.
ZEPHANIAH 3:1-2 NIV

❋ ❋ ❋

Are you a free spirit who resents correction and wants to do things your own way? In America, where independence rules, we can become too independent, too caught up in our own ways.

That kind of attitude creates a difficult worker. When an employee expects the boss to explain every decision, resents being told how to do things, or tries to change every way of doing them, the workplace becomes a stressed place. Not that workers should never question the boss or try to find a better way to work, but they also need to comply with the leaders' plans.

God connects a rebellious attitude that rejects obedience with a lack of trust in Him. When we believe He is at work in our jobs, we can trust that even the bad decisions can be retooled to improve the workplace—that even if it isn't done our way, it can be done well.

Don't follow Jerusalem's example. Instead, accept your boss's correction and that of God. Show obedience instead of rebellion.

Lord, I want to obey You on the job.
Help me be graciously obedient.

OUR PROVISION

*And Jesus answered him, saying, It is written, That man
shall not live by bread alone, but by every word of God.*

LUKE 4:4

* * *

Jesus uses bread to symbolize the edibles that sustain life. He
compares our need to take in the cereal, milk, bread, ham and
cheese, and chicken with veggies to our desperate need for God.
Without food, our lives would end, but without God's Word, our
spirits also fast and die.

We often think we're depending on our bosses to provide for
our needs. We ask for a raise or object to the one we got because
we feel we need more money to pay the bills, raise our families, or
put bread (and other things) on the table. When our bosses fail us,
we feel disappointed. Yet if they deny us, God still will not—His
Word promises His care. As we obey His truths, He provides even
for those physical needs. Even when there's only a crust of bread
in the larder, we can always depend on Him.

*Lord, thank You for caring for me even when I'm not sure
my boss does. How glad I am that You're always there.*

RIGHTEOUSNESS AT WORK

*"If a righteous person turns from their
righteousness and does evil, they will die for it."*

EZEKIEL 33:18 NIV

* * *

Righteousness isn't just a once-and-for-all thing. You can't accept Jesus then simply ignore Him for the rest of your life. If you expect to do that and still want all the benefits of heaven, you're just kidding yourself.

Treating righteousness that way would be like going to a job interview, getting the job, and never showing up for work. Who among us would expect to receive a regular paycheck if we did that? What company would last a day allowing "employees" to take such advantage of it?

God doesn't allow people to take advantage of Him, either. Those who don't show up for His kingdom day by day don't get the reward of the ones who are there working in His fields each and every day. The true believer who walks away from His commandments may receive heaven, but he'll pay a price for disobedience.

You know what it means to show up at the job every day. Do the same for God. Show His love in action at work, home, or wherever you go.

*Lord, not because I think I can earn heaven,
but because I love You, I want to seek righteousness
each day. Help me start at this moment.*

HE WALKS WITH YOU

Moses my servant is dead; now therefore arise, go over this
Jordan, thou, and all this people, unto the land which
I do give to them, even to the children of Israel.

JOSHUA 1:2

❋ ❋ ❋

No sooner had Joshua received the position of Israel's leadership than God set him a large task. The inexperienced leader was to take the people into the promised land. Surely he remembered the problems Moses had when he was last in this place. No one could have blamed Joshua for feeling a little nervous.

But Joshua was not going in alone. Not only did he have the hordes of people who made up the Hebrews, God promised to give them the land (v. 6). He would be with them as they walked into this new land. And what God promised, He did.

Are you facing something new? Does fear enter your heart at what you're taking on? We all have fears when starting a new job, getting a promotion, or making a change. But if it's something God has brought into our lives, we can count on Him to see us through. He will bring us into the blessings of our new land, as long as we obey His will.

Thank You, Lord, for this new blessing.
I trust You to help me use it wisely.

KEEP IN TOUCH

Having many things to write unto you, I would not
write with paper and ink: but I trust to come unto you,
and speak face to face, that our joy may be full.

2 JOHN 12

* * *

Some people have had a powerful impact on your career. A mentor has shown you the ropes, but you've moved on from that first job, and keeping in touch is difficult.

John knew what separation from loved ones was like. He'd probably taught this "elect lady" (v. 1) whom he wrote to, and she and her family had won a place in his heart. Being apart made communication difficult, and perhaps John was nervous about putting his thoughts on paper, since this letter was likely to be read publicly and word would be passed on to the deceivers who were undoubtedly impacting the woman's church (v. 7).

John had to travel many miles to see the woman again. Though you might like to visit your friend, travel is not your only option. Drop her an e-mail. Pick up the phone and give him a call. You may not speak face-to-face, but the communion you have can still make your joy full.

Lord, thank You for my work friend.
Bless my friend and help us keep in touch.

THINK, THEN SPEAK

*Likewise, the tongue is a small part of the body,
but it makes great boasts. Consider what a
great forest is set on fire by a small spark.*

JAMES 3:5 NIV

* * *

Damaging a promising career may not take much. Open your mouth and publicly complain about your boss, pass on some gossip, or give a client misinformation, and you can find yourself looking for a new job. That's why James warned his fellow Christians about the tongue and its dangers.

Do you think and immediately speak? Then wisdom escaped you. God's Word gives many warnings about our words and the way they impact others and our faith.

A thoughtful Christian checks on his thoughts before he opens his mouth. Will saying this harm someone? Will it wrongly portray a person's motives? Is it simply not true? Is it wishful thinking? If any of those questions can be answered yes, it's time to remain silent. No matter how much he desires to speak out, he'll hold his tongue.

So instead of speaking out boldly, check your thoughts at the door of your lips. If what you have to say is something God would call good, open up and speak.

---

*Lord, help me check my words before my lips open.
I don't want to hurt anyone with my speech.*

COMPASSION EXTENDED

*Shouldest not thou also have had compassion on
thy fellowservant, even as I had pity on thee?*

MATTHEW 18:33

* * *

If you've ever worked for a compassionate boss when your life was
filled with stress, you recognize what a blessing this attribute is.

But compassion is not wimpiness. Supporting a person through
a trial doesn't equate with a lack of accountability, as the man in
this parable learned. He'd been in debt, and his master forgave what
he owed. In turn, the greedy servant tried to extract every penny
from other servants who owed him some cash. When his master
found out about it, he was extremely angry that the servant had
not passed on a similar mercy.

We need to have compassion and respect it when it's given
to us. For a time, we receive an unusual grace, but we cannot take
advantage. That would be like taking for granted the mercy God has
given us in saving us—which is what this parable is about, after all.
God gave us His grace, and we are simply to pass it on in all things.

*Lord, thank You for forgiving me. Let me extend Your
compassion to others so they, too, can understand Your love.*

CHANGE IN PERSPECTIVE

And there we saw the giants, the sons of Anak,
which come of the giants: and we were in our own
sight as grasshoppers, and so we were in their sight.

NUMBERS 13:33

❀ ❀ ❀

The ten fearful spies who joined Caleb on the trip into Canaan may have had what we'd call a poor self-image. Compared to the Canaanites, they seemed to be small potatoes—grasshoppers even! And they imagined that their enemies would see them as these irritating insects. When the Israelite spies described themselves that way, they were relying on their own power. And looking at it from that perspective, they were probably right. They didn't have the ability to overthrow people who had cities and villages in Canaan. The Canaanites were entrenched in the land, and moving them out was a big project.

Unlike Caleb and Joshua, these men didn't consider doing the job under God's power. They forgot who had led them there and what He'd promised them.

When you feel like a grasshopper compared to coworkers, huge projects, or anything else, are you looking at yourself through the right lens? Are you seeing your working life through God's eyes or your own?

Lord, lead me in my working life. I know You've brought
me here for a reason, and I want to fulfill Your will.

TROUBLES AREN'T FOREVER

Is the seed yet in the barn? yea, as yet the vine,
and the fig tree, and the pomegranate, and the olive tree,
hath not brought forth: from this day I will bless you.

HAGGAI 2:19

* * *

God had not forgotten His covenant with His people, and He wanted to bless them as they put their disobedience behind them. The lack of food they'd suffered through ended.

When we face trials, they may feel endless. *Tomorrow will be like today, and how will we get through this?* we ask ourselves. We're tempted to feel depressed over our situations.

But nothing that's not eternal lasts forever if we make a good change. The famine ended, and so do our problems. What seems forever isn't, because situations alter. The economy improves, management is revamped, or we discover a new, better way to work. Solutions appear for most things.

Troubles don't last, but the blessings God gives do. When the figs and pomegranates are gone, the care He provided is still a warm memory that draws us ever closer to Him. He wants to bless us today with all kinds of good things. All we need to do is obey.

Lord, as I obey, I know You will bless me. Yet the
best blessing I will ever have is the joy of Your love.

MORE THAN MONEY

But godliness with contentment is great gain.
1 TIMOTHY 6:6

＊　＊　＊

Are you content with your job? Does it pay you enough to live on and maybe a little extra? Do you enjoy the work? Then don't give it up for a job that pays better but won't bring you much satisfaction and may put you at odds with God. Money isn't the only reason you work.

Godliness and contentment go hand in hand. If you don't like your job or can't pay your bills, God doesn't say you shouldn't change to a new field or get some more education so you can move up in the field you're already in.

But looking for more money isn't the only reason to find different work. Unlike many businesspeople, God doesn't make money the greatest reason for doing anything. Instead He warns against the desire to get rich and says it may become a trap leading to destruction. Some jobs pay well but force you to do things that aren't good for your spiritual life. There's no way any Christian should take on such work.

So do all you can to be successful and happy in your work, but don't only work for the cash. It's a sure way to lose your contentment.

Lord, help me find contentment and godliness in my work.

A PERFECT FOUNDATION

"He is the Rock; his deeds are perfect. Everything he
does is just and fair. He is a faithful God who
does no wrong; how just and upright he is!"

DEUTERONOMY 32:4 NLT

*   *   *

Did you learn your job from someone who was really skilled at it?
Maybe it was challenging at first to see how easily your mentor
could do things you struggled through. But after a while, you gained
skill and it became second nature to do the work. Though you may
still have hard days, you've developed competence.

No matter how effective we become at our jobs, few of us
would claim we're perfect at them (and those who do claim it should
probably be reading a devotion on lying today). But there is one
who never makes a mistake in His work, always treats everyone
fairly, and faithfully never does wrong.

Before you start feeling threatened, recognize that He's rooting
for you. He's not condemning your work, but coming alongside
you to help you do better.

Believers in Jesus are standing on this perfect Rock. What
better foundation could there be?

Lord, I want to become more like You,
on the job and off. Please bless my work.

REAL SUCCESS

*And the Lord make you to increase and abound in love one
toward another, and toward all men, even as we do toward you.*
1 THESSALONIANS 3:12

* * *

According to the stories told by Corrie ten Boom, most people wouldn't have called her father a prosperous businessman. Though Casper ten Boom was a gifted watchmaker, to him, being a successful Christian was more important than running a successful shop, and that's where he put more of his effort.

Casper didn't get any awards for the businessman who made the most money. But he was loved in the community. And better than that, he raised a family who loved God and served Him throughout their lives. During World War II, because of their faith, the family hid Jews in their home. Though they suffered greatly for it, they were faithful to God's call to help His chosen people.

Truly, love abounded in Casper ten Boom's life; it increased in his family and through the mission to the Jews. From one tiny home in Holland, Corrie became a missionary sharing God's love with the world, telling the story of her family's life and faith. And love abounded toward all.

*Lord, I want to be a successful Christian.
Show me how to be just that.*

GOD'S LEADERSHIP

" 'As a shepherd seeks out his flock on the day he
is among his scattered sheep, so will I seek out
My sheep and deliver them from all the places
where they were scattered on a cloudy and dark day.' "

EZEKIEL 34:12 NKJV

❋ ❋ ❋

Lost and scattered people covered Israel, just like sheep. On a dark day, when selfish leaders controlled the people, God suddenly acted. He gathered the people together and began leading them Himself.

If you're a follower, one of those cogs in the wheel that makes a company work efficiently, remember that even when your bosses fail you, God has not. He is still the leader you follow, and if everything seems to be falling apart, He's still in charge. He can lead where no human can. He knows the future and what guidance you need.

When you feel lost and scattered, when life no longer makes sense, turn to Jesus. Ask for His leadership for yourself. Then ask that your boss will come to understand His leadership and begin to lead in a way that will glorify Him.

Then your future will be incredibly secure, no matter what happens to your job.

Lord, I want You to lead me wherever I need
to go in life. Help my boss follow You, too.

GOOD SHEPHERDS

*I will feed them in a good pasture, and upon the high mountains
of Israel shall their fold be: there shall they lie in a good fold,
and in a fat pasture shall they feed upon the mountains of Israel.*

EZEKIEL 34:14

* * *

Notice that in all this talk of sheep and shepherds in Ezekiel 34,
you only hear about the shepherd's care for the sheep. Surely he
also got hungry, needed to do laundry, or wanted some time with
his friends. Fighting off wild animals and tracking down lost sheep
was tiring work; yet despite these needs, the good shepherd places
a priority on his valuable animals making it to the fold at night
and grazing in good fields by day.

If you're in charge, are you being a good shepherd, taking
good care of your company and its people? Or are you so busy
building a name for yourself, or covering yourself in case you get
in trouble, that you never have time to care for others?

If your people and company are valuable to you, do your best
to give them fat green fields and keep them in a good fold (or
office). Do that, and when the Good Shepherd reviews your work,
He'll be pleased.

Lord, show me how to be Your good shepherd.

REMAIN FAITHFUL

*"No one here has more authority than I do. He has held back
nothing from me except you, because you are his wife. How could
I do such a wicked thing? It would be a great sin against God."*

GENESIS 39:9 NLT

* * *

Tempted by Potiphar's wife, Joseph cried a firm "No!" Then he
explained why in these heartfelt words. His master had placed
great trust in him. He would not betray him in such a way. Even
more important, Joseph would never betray God. His Lord clearly
defined right and wrong, and Joseph understood this was wrong.

Taking God's side in the office may not be popular. Sometimes
it gets faithful believers in more trouble than if they'd just gone
along with the flow. But in the end, like Joseph, they are blessed
for their fidelity.

So when anyone tempts you to fudge on the paperwork,
approve of some seemingly small wrongdoing, or wink at a misdeed,
beware! It would be a sin against your Lord, and one that may
someday come back to bite you. Remember instead the trust your
company and God place in you, and do the right thing.

*Lord, no matter what the temptation,
help me remain faithful to Your truths.*

TACTFUL

Then Queen Esther answered, "If I have found favor with you,
Your Majesty, and if it pleases you, grant me my life—this is
my petition. And spare my people—this is my request."

ESTHER 7:3 NIV

❖ ❖ ❖

Queen Esther knew the value of tact when she approached her husband, King Xerxes. Though he seemed to approve of her, the queen understood she was asking about a serious matter, one that touched his favored counselor, Haman. So instead of barging into discussion of the issue, she invited both men to dine with her. (You might call this a business dinner.) Rather than demanding her rights as queen, she tactfully petitioned the king.

Do you demand things from your boss as if he owed them to you, or do you treat him with more respect? Are your words tactful or irritating?

Like Esther, you'll quickly find that tact receives a better response. Your boss and other managers enjoy receiving respect as much as you do and are more likely to say yes to it than to rude demands. Remember, honey always draws people better than vinegar!

Lord, ensure my words are always tactful when I speak.
Give me gracious words whenever I open my mouth.

AUTHORITY FROM ABOVE

*Samuel said, "Is it not true that even though
you were small (insignificant) in your own eyes,
you were made the head of the tribes of Israel?"*

1 SAMUEL 15:17 AMP

❀ ❀ ❀

God took a humble man and made him king!

Too bad Saul didn't stay small in his own opinion. As his authority grew, the king got a swelled head; his theme song became "My Way." He forgot that God gave him power and could take it away. Although Saul attacked the Amalekites as God commanded, the king did not also kill all the people and destroy all they owned, as God had told him to. Saul kept the pagan king alive, along with all his best livestock. As a result, God removed His blessing from Saul, and the king's story begins to become a tragedy.

Perhaps being small in our own sight isn't such a bad thing. Pride and arrogance are not Christian virtues; and when they become the hallmarks of our careers, we may quickly follow in Saul's path. Instead of success, trouble marks our footsteps. Things never go as smoothly when we walk without God.

Authority without God isn't worth much.

*Lord, any authority I have comes from You.
Help me use it wisely.*

A TIME TO SPEAK

*Give not that which is holy unto the dogs, neither cast
ye your pearls before swine, lest they trample them
under their feet, and turn again and rend you.*

MATTHEW 7:6

* * *

Did you know there are times when sharing your faith might not
be the right thing to do? God wants you to let others know about
Him, but He doesn't say you have to keep battering at people who
show no response to His good news.

If you work with antagonistic people who mock you for
believing in Jesus, your best response might be to keep your
mouth shut for a while and instead pray for the Spirit to work in
your coworkers.

When you do get around to sharing your faith with an open
heart, be certain you do it on a break, not on company time. Don't
cut into the work your boss expects of you in order to witness and
think God will still bless it. Though He wants people to hear the
good news, He also wants you to give your boss a full day.

Witnessing to faith needs to be done with wisdom as well as
fervor. Without both, you're going nowhere fast.

---

*Lord, let my heart know when You want me to open
my mouth and when I need to quietly pray for another.*

CERTAIN REWARD

By faith Moses. . .chose to be mistreated along with the people of God rather than to enjoy the fleeting pleasures of sin. He regarded disgrace for the sake of Christ as of greater value than the treasures of Egypt, because he was looking ahead to his reward.

HEBREWS 11:24-26 NIV

⊛ ⊛ ⊛

Today's reward—or tomorrow's? That's what Moses had to weigh when he gave up the palace in Egypt for mistreatment with his own people. He made a hard choice that seemed to spell disaster for his future.

We, too, have to make seemingly disastrous decisions sometimes: when we don't take the promotion we're offered because we know we won't like the job; when we encourage the company to make a choice that is right, even if it won't be as profitable as the wrong one; when we stand up for someone who's made a mistake.

We may lose earthly treasure to follow God. Like Moses, though, we still look forward to a reward—some of us in our earthly jobs, while others will see no benefit this side of heaven. But all of us will be blessed, and the heavenly recompense will be better than any under the sun.

Lord, I want to choose Your will over anything else.
Give me the faith to always stand for You.

JUSTICE FOR ALL

And David reigned over all Israel; and David
executed judgment and justice unto all his people.

2 SAMUEL 8:15

* * *

Dropped in a seemingly unimportant spot, this verse is not as minor as its placement might make it seem. In fact, it sets the tone for David's rule of Israel. In the next chapter, the writer tells a tale that proves David's concern for ruling well. After Saul and Jonathan's death, the new king asked after their households. In a surprising moment, he offered a high honor to Jonathan's only surviving son, Mephibosheth. Though most rulers would hesitate at dealing with a possible contender for the throne with anything but a sword, David showed compassionate justice toward his enemy's grandson.

Though he had his faults, at moments like this David is a wonderful example for leaders, and God blessed him for his right acts.

God does bless good leaders. As long as they follow Him, they and their followers receive many benefits. Business leaders can benefit from that truth as much as leaders of a nation.

Whether you lead a large staff or are only a small part of it, are you concerned about justice and right judgment? If so, you're a real leader.

Lord, make me a real leader who
wants to be just and judge rightly.

MAKE THE GRADE

I do not think I am in the least inferior to those "super-apostles."

2 CORINTHIANS 11:5 NIV

* * *

Imagine, the Corinthians didn't think Paul was much of an apostle! They preferred other men, whom the apostle sarcastically refers to as "super-apostles." The problem was these guys weren't really super, nor were they apostles—they were heretics, spreading lies instead of the Gospel.

Could the Corinthians have been more misled? Paul's ministry brought the Gospel to the Western world, while we don't even know the names of those not-so-super-apostles. It's hard to imagine why the Corinthians were so blind.

People don't always make right judgments about another's abilities. Perhaps a boss doesn't like an effective worker's personality or his irritating habit rubs her the wrong way. A lot can get in the way of a clear judgment.

But the final decision on who is really a good worker isn't a boss—it's God. Though you might not be a good public speaker (neither was Paul, by his own account [v. 6]), you may tell your bosses a truth others wouldn't dare share. You may encourage doing good things others avoid.

To God, obedience to Him creates a good worker.

---

*Lord, I'm no apostle, but I always want
to work for You. Show me what to do.*

BY GRACE

But by the grace of God I am what I am, and His grace toward
me was not in vain; but I labored more abundantly than they all,
yet not I, but the grace of God which was with me.

1 CORINTHIANS 15:10 NKJV

＊ ＊ ＊

Why do kids get sick enough to need a doctor's care only on days when we have to be in the office? Or the hot-water heater or dishwasher goes, and the repairman can only come on a crazy-hectic day.

These are times when God's grace needs to work overtime in our lives. If it doesn't, we're crabby to others, we race around like mad, and nothing much gets done.

But once we recognize our need for help on an out-of-control day and trust in God to control things, the day goes better. It may be hectic—we'll work hard and travel to too many places—but by the end of the day we'll discover we've accomplished a lot.

Paul understood the part grace has in our lives. It fills those empty, weak spots and makes us able to take on large tasks for God. Paul needed grace to fulfill his ministry, and we need it to do God's will in our lives.

Lord, I need Your grace every day,
but especially on the busy ones.
Please fill me now.

NEVER STOPPED

"The king should know that we went to the construction site of the Temple of the great God in the province of Judah. It is being rebuilt with specially prepared stones, and timber is being laid in its walls. The work is going forward with great energy and success."

EZRA 5:8 NLT

* * *

When God wants something done and the people doing the work are dedicated to Him, no matter what troubles arise along the way, the work is successful. The Jews rebuilding the temple learned this. Even though they had to guard against their enemies, who resented the rebuilding, the work went on. So the enemies resorted to sending this report to the king.

It's the same with your work, whatever you do. If God's in the work, you may offend some people. They may try to stop you with petty problems or bad attitudes. But if you're working for God, He will support you. You may be slowed down on occasion, but you won't be stopped. Every day, if you ask, He'll give you strength to go on and complete more than you expected.

You can go forward, with energy and success.

Lord, I want to be a success for You and through Your power. Show me how.

WISDOM FOR THE ASKING

And the king said, Divide the living child in two, and give
half to the one, and half to the other. Then spake the woman
whose the living child was unto the king... O my lord, give
her the living child, and in no wise slay it. But the other said,
Let it be neither mine nor thine, but divide it.

1 KINGS 3:25-26

❊ ❊ ❊

Solomon asked God for wisdom, and God gave it to him. The scriptures illustrate this with an amazing example of how the king used his gift from God.

Two women came to him, each claiming that a child was hers. The king, with no real knowledge of the situation, had to choose a mother for the boy. In a flash of inspiration, the king demanded that the boy be cut in half. Naturally the real mother refused, offering to give up the child so he could live. The king knew to choose this woman.

Don't you wish you had such wisdom? Remember, Solomon didn't inherit it, wise as his father, David, was. Solomon got it from God.

Today, as you face questions and decisions, you, too, can ask God for wisdom. He'll be pleased to give it to you so you can benefit others.

Lord, please give me wisdom so I can serve You better.

WELL SEASONED

Be wise in the way you act toward outsiders; make the most of
every opportunity. Let your conversation be always full of grace,
seasoned with salt, so that you may know how to answer everyone.

COLOSSIANS 4:5-6 NIV

* * *

Do you use salt in your conversations with non-Christians? That
does not mean you should say anything improper, but that your
words to nonbelievers should taste good to them. God wants
people who can share His love in a way that appeals to those who
don't know Him. How would they want to meet Him, otherwise?

What seasonings cover your words? Love, hope, compassion?
Or do yours taste of judgment, bitterness, and divisiveness? God
doesn't expect Christian speech to be dull and boring. He wants
us to have some spice to our talk, but not the kind that burns and
hurts others. Salt is a cleanser as well as a flavoring that makes
the most of food. So a believer's words should both clean hurting
hearts and bring out the best in them.

Speak wisely to those who share your working hours but not
your faith. Let salt, not chili peppers, season your words as you
share God's truth with love.

Lord, I want to speak with well-seasoned
words that draw all listeners to You.

KNOW WHAT TO WORK FOR

"Has not the LORD Almighty determined that the
people's labor is only fuel for the fire, that the
nations exhaust themselves for nothing?"

HABAKKUK 2:13 NIV

* * *

What are you really working for? Money, fame, power? Then in the end, you'll be left with empty hands. God describes your work as fuel for the fire, efforts that lead nowhere because all they gain are ashes in the end.

So why work at all? Because one day, the earth will be filled with the knowledge of God's glory (v. 14). One day everyone, believer or not, will be able to understand that God was all He claimed to be. They'll also be able to see that the witness you gave to His power and love was true.

So when you're working at the office or building whatever gadgets you make, do your best. But don't do it because money, paperwork, or gadgets are important. Do it because through you, someone might learn how wonderful Jesus is. That's the work that won't be burned by fire or exhaust you for nothing.

Lord, I always want to work for You. No matter
what my job, show me how to serve You best.

HUMBLE IN SPIRIT

Better it is to be of an humble spirit with the lowly,
than to divide the spoil with the proud.

PROVERBS 16:19

* * *

Do you recognize that a lot of "humble" people make your work possible? Like the cleaning people who come in at night to dust and polish or the person who carts away the garbage. Though you may never see these people, you know they exist because you don't have a thick layer of dust on your desk or a garbage pail that's overflowing.

In many companies, the humble people don't get much recognition or pay, but they're still important. Wait until your cleanup staff goes on strike or a key worker is out ill, and you'll know just how much they matter. Recognize how important they are, and if you can, thank them for their work.

Then take their example, and instead of getting in on all the goodies the proud folks in your office offer, side with the lowly—and God.

Lord, being humble isn't always attractive, but I know
it's what You want me to be. Help me be willing to
side with the lowly, if that's where You are.

CALM AMID ANGER

If a ruler's anger rises against you, do not leave your post;
calmness can lay great offenses to rest.

ECCLESIASTES 10:4 NIV

* * *

Has your boss become angry with you? Don't quiver in fear or become angry. Though your manager may have more experience or expertise, you're working for a human. Misunderstandings happen, but they can also be corrected.

So face an angry leader with calmness and a willingness to make things right. Instead of fixing blame, take aim at the problem. People who become angry or fearful don't do anyone a favor. The problem's still at hand. But often one calm head who's willing to take the heat off others can change a conversation's direction. What began in anger can end in peace.

Solomon knew the truth of this because he ruled over people. He probably had his mad days, when no one seemed to serve him properly. But obviously he'd also experienced the peace brought on by a faithful servant who showed calmness under pressure.

So if another is angry, keep the peace with a few calm words.

Lord, keep me peaceful when others' dander is up.

GOOD SPEAKS LOUDER. . .

For it is God's will that by doing good you should
silence the ignorant talk of foolish people.

1 PETER 2:15 NIV

* * *

Hold your tongue, speak wisely, and you'll still have a few people who don't return the favor. Once in a while, you'll hear that someone has slandered you, doubted you, or misunderstood your reasoning. In an instant, you may want to respond in kind.

Whether the issue is your faith or your work performance, take a deep breath, bite your tongue, and deal with the problem peaceably. Do all you can not to fire up the situation with harsh words or deeds. Instead, return kindness for evil and faith for doubt. Do the best you can in the situation.

By answering responsibly or even by ignoring a small, meaningless wrong, you'll gain the respect of your bosses and coworkers. Eventually, the talkers will fall silent because they recognize their misdeeds or get nowhere with them. The wrong will turn to right as your good deeds silence the foolish ones.

Lord, I want to see Your good triumph in every situation.
Help me be part of it by holding my tongue when I need to.

FRIENDLY DIFFERENCES

A friend loveth at all times,
and a brother is born for adversity.

PROVERBS 17:17

* * *

If your boss is also your friend, count yourself blessed. But also accept that at times she's going to make decisions you'll wish she hadn't made. Though you agree in many things, there will be some choices you would have made differently, for whatever reason. Those differences of opinion could destroy your friendship, if you let them.

But if you recognize that she has the position of authority and accept that, your friendship can stand firm. After all, if you were the boss, you'd get to make the decisions, but if you were wrong, you'd also get the flak. She makes her own choices and stands firm in them. If she makes a mistake, it's her responsibility, not yours.

If you truly are your boss's friend, you'll recognize that even people who disagree on some things can remain friends. You'll give her the kind of leeway you'd give any friend whose personal choices aren't your own. Though you might offer a suggestion on occasion, you won't take every different decision as a personal affront.

Love your friend faithfully, no matter what her position.

Lord, I'm glad my boss is my friend.
Let me always treat that friendship wisely.

GOD-DETERMINED

And when they had received it, they murmured against the
goodman of the house, Saying, These last have wrought
but one hour, and thou hast made them equal unto us,
which have borne the burden and heat of the day.

MATTHEW 20:11-12

＊　＊　＊

In this work-dispute parable, the workers complained to the man who hired them: they'd worked all day for the same wages as men who came later in the day; it wasn't fair. The employer objected that the early morning workers were greedy.

Jesus wasn't saying employers should treat their workers unfairly. But if a worker has a sick child, and your boss helps him out by giving him some time off with pay, don't become jealous. Be thankful, instead, that if it were you in his shoes, you might get help, too.

But Jesus wasn't really talking about the workplace when He told this story. He wanted believers to realize that the things they thought "earned" them a good place in heaven didn't. God determines heavenly value.

So if you start feeling jealous about another worker, remember this parable, and be thankful that God saved you and will give you a place in heaven.

Lord, I don't want to be jealous of the benefits You give others.
I just want to thank You for saving me.

IN GOD'S HANDS

Look! The wages you failed to pay the workers who mowed
your fields are crying out against you. The cries of the
harvesters have reached the ears of the Lord Almighty.

JAMES 5:4 NIV

* * *

If your company shortchanges you come raise time, do you feel
as if God doesn't care or is ignoring a great wrong? It's not so,
according to this verse. God knows every wrongdoing in every
corporation in the world. Even if the laborers haven't said a word,
the wrong has reached God's ears.

God promises that the rich one who defrauds the poor will
howl with miseries (v. 1). It may not be today, but eventually God
will make all even.

Does that mean you should start watching out for the howling?
Should you react in a way that will make your boss miserable? No,
God leaves revenge to Himself, and when He uses it, He uses it
wisely. But the Christian who has been wronged should respond
graciously, leaving everything in God's hands. Perhaps this wrong
will become an opportunity for God to make things right in a big
way. Those pennies you missed today could be a key to tomorrow's
success if you leave it all in His hands.

Lord, keep me from vengeful thoughts,
and help me trust in You alone.

HOLINESS AND THE WORKPLACE

God's will is for you to be holy, so stay away from all sexual sin....
Anyone who refuses to live by these rules is not disobeying human
teaching but is rejecting God, who gives his Holy Spirit to you.

1 THESSALONIANS 4:3, 8 NLT

* * *

You've heard the excuses and explanations for romantic relationships outside of wedlock. Almost undoubtedly you've worked with someone who lived with a girlfriend or became romantically involved with someone who wasn't her husband.

Just because your coworkers do it doesn't mean that avenue is open to you. If you have accepted Jesus, He wants you to be holy, set apart from the rest of the world, and that set-apartness includes your romantic life.

God's rule may seem kind of strict. You may wish you could join the crowd without offending Him. But the apostle makes it perfectly clear: those who fall into sexual sin aren't just rejecting a rule, they're rejecting God.

God's demand for holiness isn't just for His benefit; it's for ours, too. So live in a holy way and enjoy His Spirit daily.

Lord, thank You for letting me live in Your Spirit
instead of sin. Give me grace to be holy for You.

FEAR IN THE GOOD

[Joshua and Caleb] spake unto all the company of the children of Israel, saying, The land, which we passed through to search it, is an exceeding good land. If the Lord delight in us, then he will bring us into this land, and give it us; a land which floweth with milk and honey.

NUMBERS 14:7–8

* * *

God had only good things in mind for the Israelites: Before them lay a good land, one that would sustain the people with rich crops. In His generosity, God planned to give them everything they needed and more.

But right on the border, most of the Israelites felt determined to go back to Egypt into certain slavery. Suddenly, an easy trip back to food and "peace" looked better than the battle to gain the land.

We've known fear in the face of good things, too. The company is going like gangbusters, but the new hire could compete with us—and maybe we'll lose out. We're up for a raise, but will the boss remember one mistake that marred our year's performance? Like Caleb and Joshua, we can trust in God. We know He delights in us and will bring us to just the right place in His will.

Now, *will* we really trust Him?

Lord, take fear away and help me trust You.

IT'S HARD WORK

"By the sweat of your brow will you have food to eat until you
return to the ground from which you were made. For you
were made from dust, and to dust you will return."

GENESIS 3:19 NLT

◉ ◉ ◉

If Adam had known how hard work would become after he sinned, he might have thought twice about disobeying God. Pulling all those weeds and tilling hard soil took a lot more effort than caring for the garden had taken before the Fall.

Even if we don't have agricultural jobs, we can relate. Perhaps because sin infiltrated everything, all work became chores after Adam fell. Even when we enjoy the kind of work we do, we have days when we struggle to keep going. The weeds of discouragement and doubt creep into our work environment. Tasks that should have been no big problem can become full-time irritants.

Work shows us the harshness of sin and the harm it causes even those forgiven in Christ. Though Christians return to dust, just like everyone else, we serve Jesus from 9:00 a.m. to 5:00 p.m., as well as from 5:01 p.m. to 8:59 a.m. Work may be hard, but it has results if we do it for Jesus. We're also earning that eternal reward.

Lord, even when work's hard, may it be a blessing from You.

THANK GOD!

In every thing give thanks: for this is the
will of God in Christ Jesus concerning you.

1 THESSALONIANS 5:18

* * *

Difficult days are best handled by God. Over and over, that truth becomes apparent when you offer up your day to God and suddenly the irritation is eased or a light appears at the end of the tunnel for that "insoluble" problem.

But when the day works out because you've prayed briefly (though perhaps frequently), do you take the credit for yourself, or do you recognize why it worked out in the end and thank the one who smoothed the way for you?

Not thanking God is a terrible oversight—and one that may be terribly easy to do. Remembering to thank God in an impossible situation, as when a loved one is so ill the doctors can't help, isn't hard. We recognize our limitations and quickly thank Him when we hear the good news of healing. But a heart that's open to Him gradually recognizes His hand in everything, even the small things He encouraged us to have a part in.

So when your day goes better than expected, thank Him. He's always glad to hear words from a grateful heart.

Lord, thank You for making every day a better one.
Just knowing You eases my entire life.

FOREVER FOCUSED ON GOD

Woe to them that go down to Egypt for help; and stay
on horses, and trust in chariots, because they are many;
and in horsemen, because they are very strong; but they
look not unto the Holy One of Israel, neither seek the LORD!

ISAIAH 31:1

* * *

It's easy in the business world to trust in the wrong things. A huge corporation becomes your client, and everything seems great. But when you send out the billing, that company refuses to pay for months, and suddenly your company is strapped for cash. Especially if you work for a small business, that kind of problem can make a big difference.

Wise leaders don't put all their emphasis on a single client, or even a couple of them, because if those companies fail, they can, too. Having a broader view is better, in the long run, for any business.

When times are good and a client seems strong, it's hard not to trust in what you have at hand and think it could never go away. But all things on earth can disappear—only God does not change. So even when the economy is booming, don't forget to look to God, who always pays you on time and never fails.

Lord, keep me and my bosses trusting in You.

MIGHT BUT NOT RIGHT

Therefore thus saith the Lord God unto them; Behold, I, even I, will judge between the fat cattle and between the lean cattle. Because ye have thrust with side and with shoulder, and pushed all the diseased with your horns, till ye have scattered them abroad.

EZEKIEL 34:20-21

* * *

The fat animals took advantage of the weak ones—that's God's way of describing how the powerful people took advantage of the poor but faithful.

You've probably seen such things going on in the office. Some people seem able to sway others to their opinions, even if they aren't right. While an average worker may have a point, it may not be heard when a manager overwhelms it with inaccurate statistics. Or leaders who look only at the financial balance and ignore ethics may be heard more often than the softer voice of right.

Right doesn't always make might in the workplace; in fact, it often seems just the opposite. But just as it took God a while to correct Israel's wrongdoing, it may take Him time to bring down the wrongs in a corporate environment. That doesn't mean it won't happen or that you want to be a fat sheep when the Good Shepherd comes to the aid of the weak ones.

Lord, keep me from becoming fat on weaker sheep.

TWO ARE BETTER

Two are better than one, because they
have a good reward for their labor.
ECCLESIASTES 4:9 NKJV

* * *

Overwhelmed with work? Then take this biblical advice and get some help. It might seem incredibly obvious, but two people work faster than one.

Working together as a team may be something of a challenge. First you have to decide how to break up the work. You may be able to take a stack of papers and split them. That makes life easy. But a more complex job means you have to decide who does what and how to make decisions in both parts that will even out in the end. Communication suddenly becomes very important.

But God's all in favor of people working together. When their differences challenge them, they can learn to love each other in new ways. Deciding how to break up work and who's responsible for what makes two people move in the same direction. A shared job also has a shared goal and shared benefits. Both workers get to look forward to the same reward. If both do well, both get credit. If one does badly, both suffer. But according to God, two are still better than one.

Lord, help me work well with others when I have a job to share.

GIVE BACK

*"At the end of every third year, bring the entire tithe of that year's harvest and store it in the nearest town. . . . Then the L*ORD *your God will bless you in all your work."*

DEUTERONOMY 14:28-29 NLT

❀ ❀ ❀

Did you know God's blessing on your work doesn't only depend on what you do during the week from nine to five? The money you place in the offering plate on Sunday may have an impact on how He blesses you the rest of the week.

If you thought you could separate your church giving from the rest of your life, think again. God doesn't say that. The way you treat Him on Sunday carries over to the rest of the week. Shortchange Him on the weekend, and He won't bypass it at the week's start. When you steal from God by withholding from the offering plate, He still feels the pain on Monday morning.

Give generously to God's work—and you can expect all your work to be blessed. That's a benefit you couldn't receive from this world, even if you gave every penny of your income and everything else you own.

Lord, I give control of my money to You.
Show me how to give it to Your glory.

A ROUNDABOUT CAREER PATH

He was thirty years old when he began serving in the court of
Pharaoh, the king of Egypt. And when Joseph left Pharaoh's
presence, he inspected the entire land of Egypt.
GENESIS 41:46 NLT

* * *

Abused by his brothers, sold into slavery, lied about by a temptress, sent to jail. None of these sound like the path to becoming second-in-command of a nation. Yet each step led Joseph closer to greatness.

Our career paths may seem as checkered as Joseph's. We're out of work for a while and end up landing a less-than-perfect job. We stay in the "wrong" job too long and fear it won't look good on a résumé. We don't have a perfect education for the job we'd like and can't afford to go back to school.

But somehow, even those weaknesses in our job histories can become strengths. We are never entirely in control of our careers, any more than Joseph was, but God rules over everything. His plans will come to fruition in the end, if we follow His paths.

Lord, I have little control over my career.
Take it in Your hands and use it for Your purposes.

GOD SEES

And Samuel said unto Jesse, Are here all thy children?
And he said, There remaineth yet the youngest, and,
behold, he keepeth the sheep. And Samuel said unto Jesse,
Send and fetch him: for we will not sit down till he come hither.

1 SAMUEL 16:11

❋ ❋ ❋

None of us like to be forgotten or thought of as unimportant. We want people to respect our ideas and even seek them out. When there's an honor to be handed out, we'd like to be considered for it, whether it's a promotion or an award.

But even King David had a time when he was forgotten. Out watching sheep—a lowly job—David was out of the way. When the prophet Samuel asked Jesse to see his sons, the father forgot his youngest son. Who would imagine this boy as a king? No one in the family saw the promise in the youth who became a successful warrior and ruler.

Just because others don't see your promise, don't give up. God sees when others are blinded by their humanity. His wonderful, promise-filled future does not rely on human ideas of your value.

Even if the whole world forgets or ignores you, Jesus doesn't.

Lord, thank You for remembering me when the world forgets.

TOUCH BASE WITH GOD

Unless the LORD builds a house,
the work of the builders is wasted.

PSALM 127:1 NLT

✳ ✳ ✳

We've all worked really hard and felt as if we were getting nowhere. Not every labor turns out well, even if we're committed to the job and do our best. Sometimes it's simply a matter of things that don't fit together because someone else on the job hasn't pulled his weight.

But at other times, we've started building a house without checking our ideas with the Master Architect. He would have told us we weren't using the right building materials, were planning on building in the wrong location, or should scrap the project before we started, but we never asked. So we spend all that money and effort, only to find ourselves in trouble.

If we want to build strong houses in every area of our lives, we need to check in regularly with God about both our spiritual and "secular" houses, because we can't separate one from the other. Really, for a Christian, nothing is secular. It's all committed to our Lord. If our whole lives are entrusted to Him, we won't "forget" to ask His help, whatever we're building.

Lord, remind me to check with You
before I build anything into my life.

WHAT'S NEXT?

And they that went in, went in male and female of all flesh,
*as God had commanded him: and the L*ORD *shut him in.*

GENESIS 7:16

❋ ❋ ❋

As the door closed on Noah and his family, doubts must have filled their minds. Soon they'd be floating on the water in an ark full of animals, the only living creatures above the waves. Before them lay a lot of unknowns, and only one thing they knew for sure: God had saved them. He had a plan in this, but they hardly knew what to make of it. What would their new world be like? Where would they end up? How would they live?

We, too, face unknowns. How will the new job work out? Will we like our new coworker? What will our boss ask us to do today, next week, next year? Will we get the new account? We can tie ourselves up with what-ifs and doubts or accept that God is guiding us in this, too, and get on with the work.

Whether we're Noah or a twenty-first-century Christian, we can trust that God has saved us for a reason and live that out day by day.

Even when I don't know what's going on, Lord, I trust in You.

GOD WORKS, TOO

*"All the earth shall worship You and sing praises to You;
they shall sing praises to Your name." Come and see the works
of God; He is awesome in His doing toward the sons of men.*

PSALM 66:4-5 NKJV

* * *

You're working to please God, but did you know He's also been working for you? He gave you a beautiful world to live in, friends and family to love, and many other blessings. He also used His power to save you; He's freed you from sin and rules over your life.

But He didn't stop there. Every day, when you get up, you can count on God's protection, guidance, and the work of His Spirit to make you increasingly like His Son. He's doing a great work in you as well as working for you. Hasn't your life been changed from top to bottom? You're a new creature entirely. And He continues to work on you every day of your life, making you better and better.

When the psalmist thought of all God had done for him, he became so impressed that he just had to start praising his Lord.

Is praise rising to your lips, too?

*I praise You, Lord, for all the work
You've done for me and in me.*

If You Liked This Book,
You'll Want to Take a Look at...

Secrets of the Proverbs 31 Woman

This devotional, offering equal parts inspiration and encouragement, will uncover the "secrets" of the Proverbs 31 woman. Each reading, tied to a theme from Proverbs 31:10–31, is rooted in biblical truth and spiritual wisdom. Women of all ages will be inspired to emulate the virtues extolled in this memorable passage of scripture.
Paperback / 978-1-63058-861-8 / $12.99

Secrets of Ruth

This devotional, offering equal parts inspiration and encouragement, will uncover the "secrets" of Ruth. Each reading, tied to a theme from the Old Testament story of Ruth, the Moabitess, is rooted in biblical truth and spiritual wisdom. Women of all ages will be inspired to emulate the example of enduring love extolled in this memorable passage of scripture.
Paperback / 978-1-63409-034-6 / $12.99

Find These and More from Barbour Publishing at Your Favorite Bookstore or at www.barbourbooks.com

BARBOUR
PUBLISHING